The Best of "Lives to Inspire"

Stories for Assemblies
& Collective Worship
in School and Church

by John Godwin

MOORLEY'S Print & Publishing

British Library Cataloguing in Publication Data.
A catalogue record for this book is available
from the British Library.

Cover illustration by Greg Clifton

ISBN 0 86071 552 3

MOORLEY'S Print & Publishing
23 Park Rd., Ilkeston, Derbys DE7 5DA
Tel/Fax: (0115) 932 0643

The Best of "Lives to Inspire"

The first volume of "Lives to Inspire" has been used in schools for over twenty years, and has had widespread appeal. Subsequent "Lives" have added considerably to the range of stories suitable for Christian Morning Assemblies.

It has recently been decided to make one volume of the most popular stories in the three volumes, and this is launched in the hope that it will find equally wide appeal, for many of these stories are surely the birthright of every child. Young minds can be stirred by noble deeds, and many children have been led to lead inspired lives themselves through listening to stories of courageous men and women.

The stories may be read as they are, or - as I prefer – told to the children without the book, having first acquainted myself with the facts.

John Godwin

Stoney Stanton
Leicestershire
2001

Contents

ALBAN

Alban was a wealthy Briton who lived in a country house at a place called Verulamium in this country well over sixteen hundred years ago, at a time when Britain was a part of the Roman Empire. He worshipped heathen gods, as did most of his friends.

One day there was a knock at his door, and Alban found there an agitated old man. "Please let me in quickly!" he gasped. "The Roman soldiers are searching for me, and they will kill me if they find me."

"Why, what have you done to deserve death?" enquired Alban, motioning to the old man to enter.

"Nothing," replied the old man, "except that I am a follower of Jesus Christ, and I tell others about Him."

"Here," he said, "come this way. I'll find you a hiding place."

When the fugitive was safely hidden, Alban asked him more about Jesus Christ, and he listened for a long time as the old man, who gave his name as Amphibalus, told of his Master. Alban could see no cause for death in believing about Christ; in fact the more he heard the more he was eager to know.

The old man's story was cut short by the tramp of marching soldiers approaching Alban's gate.

"I'll leave you here; you'll be quite safe," said Alban. "But take my robe, and give me your cloak. Quickly, now!" He had suddenly been seized with a desire to protect the old man by impersonating him.

The soldiers burst into the room, and seized the man in the cloak. Only when he was dragged before the magistrates was he recognised as Alban. The magistrate tried by torture to discover where Alban had hidden the priest but he refused to tell, and therefore was condemned to death. The executioner, however, refused at the last moment to do the deed, so a soldier was found who was prepared to put to death both Alban and the official executioner.

On the spot where Alban died, the people built a little church, and they called the place St. Albans. There is still a shrine to him in St. Albans Abbey.

Because Alban had died so bravely, people wanted to know more about the cause for which he had given his life, and many of the enquirers became Christians themselves. As far as we know, Alban was the first person in Britain to die for Christ; the first British martyr. Sadly Amphibalus was captured a few days later, and, according to tradition, was stoned to death.

To think about:

If an anti-Christian enemy captured our country today, should we be prepared to stand up for Jesus, even if it led us into great danger? Or should we, like Peter in the Bible, deny knowing Jesus if we thought it would save our skin?

A Prayer:

O Lord, many of the early Christians were very brave people, and we know that in some countries today Christians have to be just as brave. Help me always to serve you as bravely as I can, and to fear no-one as long as I have You.

For further reading:

Unstead, R.J.	From Caractacus to Alfred	A. & C. Black Chapter 4
Alick, J.	A People's Book of Saints	Longmans, Green & Co. p 43 – 49
Burra, Elizabeth	Who Comes First?	Scripture Union
Cox, Lilian E.	God's Mighty Men	Religious Education Press.

THOMAS ARNOLD

In the early part of the nineteenth century there were very few schools for ordinary boys and girls. The so-called Public Schools were not public in the sense that they were free; parents had to pay for their children to go to them. But they were not very civilised educational institutions by today's standards, and it was not until Thomas Arnold came to Rugby School that changes for the better took place.

Thomas Arnold was born in the Isle of Wight in 1795. He was educated at Oxford University, and in 1820 he married. Two years earlier he had been ordained as a clergyman.

It was in 1828 that he was appointed Headmaster of Rugby Public School. At this time many people were against education in Public Schools and if one reads "Tom Brown's Schooldays" one can appreciate some of the reasons why this was so. Boys were often treated by other boys, and indeed by their masters, in a heartless and cruel way. Floggings were common, and senior boys were allowed to treat younger boys in ways no-one would tolerate today. It was thought by many that this kind of treatment toughened up the boys in readiness for the hard world into which they would be going.

But there was another view of education, in which Dr. Arnold and other enlightened men and women of his day believed. This view said that education should be based on morals and rules by which one's life should be conducted. Education must, most importantly be based upon Christian principles, said Arnold.

So he started a complete reform of the English Public School system, in which the character and the quality of the individual teachers was of the utmost importance. The tone of the school was another vital ingredient, and any boy whose influence was not desirable should be removed from the school. There must be a wise system of punishment and rewards to pupils; older boys who had proved themselves should be taught how to express themselves correctly, and how to acquire a thirst for knowledge. Every pupil must be taught to understand his responsibility to all levels of society.

Arnold made such an impression on Rugby School that others were opened along similar lines. Subjects such as history, English literature and mathematics were given top priority in the timetables of these schools.

But Arnold will be chiefly remembered for the importance he attached to Religious Education in his vision on education. He had his critics, of course, but he stands out in history as the most notable figure of modern times in secondary education.

He died suddenly on June 12th, 1842.

To think about:

What is the first task of a school? Is it to prepare children for the work they will do after their schooldays are over? Is it to aim for scholastic success in examinations? Is it to show children how they can live a life of service to others?

Should the teaching of the Christian religion form an essential part of the curriculum? If so, should it be treated more or less as history, leaving boys and girls to "take it or leave it"? Or should it be taught only by those with Christian conviction, that is by those who are convinced that Christ's life gives us the only true pattern upon which to base our lives?

What do you consider to be the really important subjects to be taught at school? Should boys be taught exactly the same subject as girls?

A Prayer:

O Lord, guide all those who teach, that they may be led by Your example, set before us by Jesus Christ our Lord. Guide, too, those who learn, that they may gain through their contact with good men and women, so that they are consequently enriched to lead useful lives in the service of others. Amen.

For further reading

Dr. Arnold of Rugby   Norman Wymer 1953
Tom Brown's Schooldays   Thomas Hughes

ROBERT BADEN-POWELL

Robert Baden-Powell, who became world famous as the Chief Scout, served his country both as a wonderful soldier and as one who strove to establish a true brotherhood of Man.

Born in Paddington, London on February 22nd, 1857, he was one of ten children of a clergyman and his wife. His Godfather was railway pioneer George Stephenson.

Mr Baden-Powell senior, a University Professor, died when Robert was only three, and after being educated at first by his mother, the young boy went to a school in Tunbridge Wells, and afterwards to Charterhouse School in Surrey. He displayed a wide range of abilities at school, though his academic work was not of a very high standard. But he showed a particular interest in Scouting, and particularly enjoyed catching rabbits in the school grounds when no-one was looking, and cooking them in the open air. On holiday, his adventurous spirit was given full scope, for he loved yachting on the south coast, and canoeing on some of the English rivers.

He proved to be a wonderful soldier and saw service in India and Africa. By the time he was 43 he was a Major General, and showed great qualities of leadership at the famous 217 day Siege of Mafeking in 1899. At this time, his famous "Aids to Scouting" was published, and a few years later he re-wrote this to appeal to young boys.

He realised more and more that his book contained much that would be of immediate appeal to the adventurous element in boys, and in 1907 he brought together 21 boys from varied backgrounds to camp on Brownsea Island in Dorset. It was an unqualified success. Next year he published "Scouting for Boys" in six fortnightly parts, and the sales exceeded his wildest expectations. Many Scouts formed themselves into groups to try out B.P.'s ideas, and the enthusiasm generated was such that the Scout movement mushroomed until it spread across the land, and, ultimately, across the British Commonwealth and to many other countries of the world.

In spite of his brilliant prospects in the Army, B.P. decided in 1910, largely on the advice of King Edward VII, to dedicate all his energies to the Scout Movement. Two years later he married Olave Soames, who eventually became Lady Baden-Powell, Chief Guide.

In 1920 the first International Scout Jamboree was held in London. At the conclusion of the great gathering, B.P. was accorded the position of Chief Scout of the world.

He was a man of wide and varied interests, for in addition to Scouting he enjoyed fishing, polo, big game hunting, painting and sculpture.

Many honours were showered upon him. He died in Africa in 1941, aged 83, and left behind him a message for all Scouts, in which he stressed that real happiness is found by serving others. In advising his Scouts to try to leave the world a better place than they found it, he concluded by asking for God's help on those who tried to do this.

To think about:

Baden-Powell was a man set for a brilliant future in the Army. But almost at the height of his career he decided to channel his interests and his talents into serving the Youth of his country. He gave them ideals for which to strive, through a programme of absorbing activities which appealed immediately to boys. Today the Movement he started stretches practically round the world. Thousands of Scouts have forged links of friendship which would not otherwise have been there. Racial and political barriers have been broken down by these friendships. In doing his great work, B.P. was conscious that he was serving God, as well as mankind.

A Prayer:

O Lord, help us to remove all barriers which divide man from man. May we always remember that all political boundaries are man-made, and that all men are created equal in your sight, no matter what may be their creed, or colour of their skin. Amen.

For further reading:
Reynolds, E.E.   Baden-Powell   O.U.P.

DOCTOR BARNARDO

Dr. Thomas John Barnardo was born in Dublin on July 4th, 1845, the son of a German immigrant whose family came originally from Spain. When he was a young man he wanted to go to China as a medical missionary, so he trained as a doctor and worked through an outbreak of cholera in London in 1865. During this period he took an intense interest in his spare time in teaching poor boys in "ragged schools".

One winter's afternoon, he was dismissing his group of boys after a school session, when one of them named James Jarvis hung back at the door, obviously not eager to go. He was barefooted, and wore few clothes apart from a ragged overcoat. "Come on, my lad", said Barnardo, "Off you go home to your father and mother."

The boy replied that he had no home, nor had he a father or mother. Barnardo thought that the boy was joking, but the look on his face at last convinced him that he was telling the truth.

"You mean you've nowhere in the world to go tonight?" he said, and after the boy had nodded, added, "And are there other boys like you, with no homes?"

The boy nodded again. "Like to see some?" he said.

Barnardo needed no second bidding, but followed the boy through a maze of narrow streets and alleyways, until they arrived at the River Thames. By a low brick wall several boys were huddled together covered in filthy old rags and newspapers. The night was bitterly cold. The Doctor's attention was caught by another group of boys who were rummaging through piles of rubbish nearby, trying to find themselves something to eat.

The Doctor was so moved by what he saw that he knew instantaneously where his life's duty now lay. He must do all he could to try to save destitute children in this country. His plans to go to China were abandoned, and he set out with a will to fulfil his self-appointed task. There could be no turning back.

By 1870 he had opened on Stepney Causeway his first home for destitute children, all taken from the streets. With money given him by well-wishes, he fed and clothed the children, and gave them a Christian education. At first, he hadn't the room to take all the children he would like to have done, and one poor boy who was asked to wait for admission for a few days was found in the street next day – dead.

Barnardo's first Homes were for boys, but homes for girls were also opened later. All the children learned a trade as part of their education, so that they could earn a useful living when they left the Homes.

When he died at Surbiton, Surrey, on September 19th, 1905, aged 60, Barnardo had saved sixty thousand children from the streets. His great work is still carried on today.

To think over:

There are still many cities in the world where homeless children roam in the back streets. What can be done for them? Would <u>we</u> be prepared, as Dr. Barnardo was, to give up a promising career in order to work for unfortunate human beings without any thought of repayment in money? Are Children's Homes still needed today? Are they as good as real homes in a family? If not, why not?

A Prayer:

Lord, we ask You to show us, as Christians, the way to do all we can for those who need our help. Make us always sensitive to the needs of others.

For further reading:

Ford, D.	Dr. Barnardo (Lives to Remember)	Black
Scott, C.	Ever Open Door: The Story of Dr. Barnardo	Lutterworth
Williams, G.	Barnardo, the Extraordinary Doctor	Macmillan
Wymer, N.	Father of Nobody's Children	Arrow Books

AAGE BERTELSEN

During World War II the German forces over-ran a number of European countries, and wherever they went the soldiers of the Third Reich, assisted by the secret police, the Gestapo, ruthlessly suppressed any opposition. The German Nazi Party had a particular hatred of the Jewish race, for their twisted thinking blamed the Jews for all Germany's economic ills after World War I. Such was the feeling of Hitler and the Nazis towards the Jews that by the end of World War II they had killed 6,000,000 of them in what much surely have been one of the greatest acts of barbarity of all time. Many wonderful stories are told of men and women, some of them Germans, who did not agree with Hitler's methods, and who did all they could, often at great personal risk, to hide Jews.

Such a man was Aage Bertelsen, one of Denmark's great heroes. Germany over-ran his country in 1940, and after leaving the Jews in peace for a short time, Hitler determined that the moment had come for them to be rounded up.

Bertelsen, a Lutheran Bible teacher and a man of profound Christian conviction, could not stand idly by while Hitler did his evil work. With some determined friends, he decided to do all he could to hide these unfortunate people. None of them knew any Jews personally, so first they had to be found.

They questioned likely-looking people in the street. If they acknowledged that they were Jews, Bertelsen and his friends invited them to stay in their houses. The method seemed simple enough, though it was fraught with danger. But it worked. Other people followed the example of these brave Danes, and many Jews were found safe hiding places.

Soon it became apparent that the only permanent solution to the problem was to get the Jews out of the country, beyond the reach of the Gestapo. So secret routes out of Denmark and across the sea to Sweden were organised. Again, the operation was perilous, for if any of the Danes had been caught by the Germans they would have faced brutal torture and almost certain death.

More than 5,000 people were thus taken to safety, and this represented over 90% of all the Jews in the country. After the War was over the refugees were all brought back to their homes again at the expense of the Government of Denmark.

This work of love and concern by this great Danish Christian and his helpers has gone on record for all time. It is all the more remarkable because the people who were saved were not personal friends of Bertelsen. He and his friends risked their lives to save their unfortunate fellow men in their hour of need.

To think about:

It is not difficult to do a good turn to those who are our friends; those we love and respect. But to do a good deed to unknown people is harder. How should we behave if we knew that people who were unknown to us were in grave danger, and if we knew that we had it in our power to help them? Suppose, for example, that one of the minority groups in this country was being persecuted, and we knew that we should run the risk of danger to ourselves if we tried to help them. What should we do? Christ showed compassion and concern for all, not just his special friends. He even had a word of comfort for the thief on the Cross, and he showed mercy and understanding to the lepers and to other outcasts of society.

A Prayer:

O God, help us we pray Thee to show concern for everyone around us, whether or not they are our friends, and no matter to what race or creed they belong. Teach us never to flinch from danger in our efforts to love our neighbour as ourselves.

For further reading:

Carlson, Betty	Happiness Is.	Lakeland

LOUIS BRAILLE

Three-year-old Louis Braille sat one day in the year 1812 on the floor of his father's workshop in the French village of Coupvray. His father made goods from leather, and the workshop floor was littered with scraps. While his father's back was turned, the young boy picked up some of his father's tools, and as he was playing with these the sharp point of a knife somehow penetrated one of his eyes. Medical help was not available, and soon the wound became infected. Before long the infection had spread to the other eye. Now it was too late. Louis Braille was blind, and nothing could be done to restore his sight.

In spite of this tragedy, Louis, a clever little boy, taught himself to do most things, and to move around with the aid of a stick. At school, he soon found he could commit to memory most of what the teacher said.

At the age of ten, he was admitted into France's only School for the Blind, which was in Paris. Here he learned to read, using special books with raised Roman letters. But the few books in the school were very clumsy to handle, and were also very heavy. Reading was a slow business. Louis soon read all that there was to read, and he set his active mind to work on the possibility of other, quicker methods of reading for blind people.

Two years later, a Captain in the French Army demonstrated at the school a system of sending messages using dots and dashes raised on the surface of a card. By this means, soldiers could interpret messages delivered at night, when naked lights were forbidden in war time. This Army code gave Louis the idea that he would try to devise a method of his own, using the same basic system. He worked on the principle of variations on a basic pattern of six dots, arranged in three rows of two, the six dots being so close together that they would all fit underneath a finger tip. By having only selected dots raised within the pattern to represent each letter, there would be adequate variations possible to make all the letters of the alphabet clearly distinguishable to the touch.

Within three years, the young Braille had completed his reading system for the blind. Throughout his experiments he was conscious of the fact that God was guiding him in his work. He tried out his code on blind people, and although at first there was considerable opposition from teachers of the blind, his method gradually proved itself to be the easiest and the best.

Louis also learned to play the organ by touch, and became a good player. Unfortunately, he died of tuberculosis at the early age of 43. After his death, his system of teaching blind people to read was brought into use all over the world. Today there are many thousands of books made in "Braille", the system which was named after its inventor.

His body now rests in a place of honour in Paris.

To think about:

Can we form any idea of what life would be like without sight and hearing? It is a good idea to make a list of things you like doing that would be impossible without (a) sight and (b) hearing. Why is it, do you think, that many blind people are happy and content? Find out all you can about the latest aids for the blind.

Have you read about some of the diseases in tropical lands that can cause blindness, and of the work of the World Health Organisation in fighting these diseases? In many cases blindness can be prevented at very low cost.

A Prayer:

Help us, O Lord, to use our senses aright; to hear and see what is worthy and noble and good in others; and help us, too, to see all those things which call for our help.

For further reading:

Christiaens, J.	Conqueror of the Night; Louis Braille	Abelard-Schuman
Kugelmass, J.S.	Louis Braille	Julian Mesner Inc. 1951
Bickel, L.	Triumph over Darkness	Allen & Unwin

JOHN BROWN

Slavery is a terrible thing. Many British people, to their eternal discredit, participated in the nefarious sale of black people who had been forcibly taken from their homes in Africa, and shipped to America in conditions of indescribable horror. Large numbers died before they reached their destination. Those who did reach America were sold in the market-place like cattle, and became the property of their white masters. The work they were given to do was tedious and monotonous, and they were usually whipped if they did not sustain their efforts.

Many white men accepted this state of affairs without a murmur. But some did not. Such a man was John Brown, born on 9th May 1800, one of a family of 16 children, in Conneticut, U.S.A. He never attended school, but learned to read from the one book in his father's house, the Bible. Here he perceived that God meant men to be brothers, and he was sure that God included black men as well as white men in His plans. Such was the conviction of Brown and of his sons that they were right in their interpretation of God's Will that they determined that they must take the law into their own hands if they were to free the slaves.

Brown knew that if only slaves could escape to Canada, where slavery had been abolished, they would be free. So he and his friends planned escape routes, with hiding places where runaway slaves would be safe as they made their bid for freedom.

But few slaves dared to take the risk. So Brown and his friends raided a slave owner's plantation, and carried off some slaves to freedom. Now there was a price on Brown's head, for in the raid some white men had been killed. Brown was not deterred, but he realised that the size of the problem was such that he must make bigger plans if the end of slavery was to be secured. So he planned to capture arms. In 1859 he set up a kind of military headquarters at Harper's Ferry. He seized the arms store at the Federal armoury there, but he was soon surrounded by Government troops under Colonel Robert E. Lee, captured, and gaoled at Charlestown, Virginia. Brown had been seriously wounded, and two of his sons had been killed. After a trial he was hanged for murder and treason. As he went to his death, he took a negro baby in his arms, and kissed it. He was buried at North Elba, New York.

Some people thought John Brown was a villain, because he had been prepared to kill in order to achieve his aims. Others, like the famous American Ralph Waldo Emerson, thought he was a hero. But whatever his shortcomings, he made America see how wrong slavery was. Two years after his death, the American Civil War broke out between the States which supported slavery and those which did not. The soldiers who fought for freedom sang as they marched along:

"John Brown's body lies a mouldering in the grave,
But his soul goes marching on!"

To think about:

Many people used to see nothing wrong in slavery. Many, even today, believe coloured people to be inferior to white people. What should we think today if, in our country, we saw coloured people being treated in a very unjust way? John Brown was prepared to kill to achieve his ends. Is it ever right to kill?

A Prayer:

Lord, sometimes we have to take a stand, even though we may be unpopular. Give us the courage to stand fast for what we know is right, and not to flinch in the face of danger.

For further reading:

Villard, Oswald	John Brown 1800-1859; A Biography Fifty Years After	Peter Smith
Graham, Lorenz	John Brown's Raid; a Picture History of the Attack on Harper's Ferry, Virginia.	School Book Service
Cox, Lilian E.	God's Mighty Men	Religious Education Press

GEORGE CADBURY

George Cadbury and his brother Richard inherited the family cocoa business in Birmingham in 1861, when only a dozen workers were employed in the firm, and when George was only twenty-two years old. Life was hard in these days, and to make ends meet the brothers had to deny themselves every luxury. A bequest from the will of their mother, who died at this time, helped to ease the burden of a business that would only just pay for itself.

The brothers were both devout Christians, and belonged to the Society of Friends, or Quakers. This group of people have a very strong sense of responsibility towards their neighbours, and George and Richard were determined that, come what may, they must pay their workpeople a decent weekly wage, and treat them with respect. They gave their employees Saturday afternoons off, a thing no-one else in Birmingham was prepared to do in those days. Business people scoffed at the way the brothers treated their employees, who were even encouraged to attend the Adult School, which George and Richard helped to pioneer in Birmingham.

But the business did not prosper, and the brothers were on the point of selling up. Richard did quit, but George, at the last minute, decided not to do so, because things began to pick up a little. He found a method of making cocoa pleasant to drink by extracting the cocoa-butter, rather than by adding flour and starch, as had been the usual practice up to this time. Soon the business was prospering, and George made a lot of money.

Now he was able to give expression to revolutionary ideas he had been turning over in his mind for some time. He would move his factory out of the grime of Birmingham, and, for the benefit of his workpeople, he would construct new buildings in the pleasant countryside surrounding the City. All round his factory he would build pleasant, well-spaced houses for his employees and others, and the whole layout would resemble a large garden. George had long been convinced that bad housing lay at the root of much social evil.

He achieved his dream in 1879. The factory and houses in the country were given the name Bournville. Cadbury's ideas on housing were widely adopted later by many town planners.

He went further by paying his employees old-age pensions, long before they were commonplace in this country.

Cadbury worked hard for the unity of the Christian Churches. In politics he was a great Liberal, and he purchased national newspapers so that his views should find widespread expression.

Shortly before he died, on 24th October 1922 his firm amalgamated with that of J.S. Fry of Bristol, and by this time 4000 workers were employed altogether.

Cadbury left behind him a pattern of industrial relations which has many times been copied, but seldom equalled.

To think about:

How far do you think a factory owner is responsible for his workpeople's welfare and happiness? If we started a business of our own, should we be content just to make money, or should we think we ought to play some part in shaping the sort of lives our workpeople led in their leisure time?

Would there be a danger that any help offered by us in this direction might be construed as interference into people's private lives, and as being paternalistic? How far is one justified in trying to influence the lives of others for good, as one sees it? Some who try to do this are called derisively "do gooders". What do you think?

A Prayer:

Lord, we know that throughout this life we are dependent on each other. Help us to play our full part, and to accept our social responsibilities.

For further reading:

Parker, Anthony   Great Men of Warwickshire   Pitman
Hayes, E.H. & Cox, L.E.   Yarns on Christian Torchbearers   R.E.P.

ELIJAH CADMAN

You may have never heard of Elijah Cadman, yet his story is a fascinating one, and shows how the spirit of man can triumph over the degradation into which worldly conditions have dragged him.

Elijah was born in Coventry in December, 1844, to very poor parents. His father often drowned his sorrows in drink, and his grandfather was killed in a public house brawl. When he was still a young boy, his father was transported to Australia for life for an offence he had committed, and Elijah was allowed to kiss his father goodbye through the prison cell bars. Mrs Cadman and the family went to the workhouse, where she was separated from the children as a matter of policy. She protested, smashed some windows, and was sent to prison for fourteen days.

Life was very hard, and Elijah started his first job when he was five years old. His maternal grandfather, thinking his education was being neglected, paid two pence a week for him to attend a Dame School, but Elijah was a spirited boy, and was soon in trouble for assaulting his teacher. For a punishment he was shut up in a small dark cavity, the only air supply for which came down a small chimney. Elijah found he could climb the chimney, and escape by scaling a wall.

It seems that his ability to climb the chimney determined the course of his future life. For when he was only five and a half years old, he and his brother, sixteen months younger, were placed in charge of Dick Carr, a sweep, to learn the trade of climbing boy. In these days, boys were often sold to sweeps for this purpose.

At first Dick fed them well, but this was merely a prelude to years of misery and cruelty. During the eleven years the boys were with Dick they received no wages. The only money they received was that which grateful people whose chimneys they had cleaned gave them. Climbing chimneys was hard, terrible work, and the remedy for the injuries received on the legs and arms from the sharp bricks of the narrow chimneys was to have salt and water rubbed in the wounds to harden them. In the depths of winter the boys were dressed only in cotton trousers and shirt, and they walked the streets barefooted. Elijah would sometimes sweep as many as sixteen chimneys a day.

At the same time, he was often in trouble with the Police for stealing, and from the age of six he was often drunk. As he grew older he spent periods of unemployment in the degradation of the workhouse.

The turning point in his life came one day when, with eight thugs who were his friends, he set out to see two men publicly hanged in Warwick. As he watched the macabre spectacle, one of his friends whispered, "You'll come to this, you know Cadman". Elijah thought long and hard upon these words.

Shortly afterwards he stopped to hear a man preaching about Christ. He was visibly moved by the message, and by the realisation, for the first time in his life, that he "stood on the brink of hell". That night he prayed, and it was for him the beginning of a new life. Eventually he found a peace such as he had never known before. He joined the Salvation Army to tell others in the streets of his new found love of God, and eventually he became Commissioner Cadman, Coventry's second officer in the Salvation Army.

To think about:

In the first half of the last century, life for many ordinary people was very humiliating and depressing. We have to thank the brave social pioneers who, in the name of Christ, picked up these broken souls and offered them a new life and a new vision in the service of God.

Read the story of Lord Shaftesbury, and of all that he did to combat the social evils of his day; and in particular his efforts to end the scandal of the climbing boys. Read, too, of the efforts of the Salvation Army to reach the "down and outs" and the rejects of society; those nobody else seemed to want.

What is it in Man that, however low he may have sunk, will respond to the call of goodness, of righteousness, and love? So many lost souls have been changed completely when touched by the Hand of God. There are some political creeds that preach that Man can be happy and fulfilled without God if only Man's material needs can be met. Can he? What is your opinion?

A Prayer:

O God, we thank You for the brave social pioneers who have battled against adversity to make a better world in which to live. But above all we thank You for sending Jesus Christ, to give us a vision of things eternal, and of a Love that never dies. Amen.

For further readings:

The details about Elijah Cadman were taken from an article in the Coventry Standard of July 3rd, 1891.

In Darkest England   William Booth 1890

KING CANUTE

There was much fighting and treachery in this country when Canute came here to rule in the eleventh century, and the King had many problems with which to contend. But he was a strong supporter of the Church, and he made at least one pilgrimage to Rome; a most desirable activity for Christians of his day.

In spite of having many shortcomings, Canute developed some of the qualities of the true Christian. Probably the best-known story about him concerns his desire to show his courtiers that he cared little for the flattery which they continually gave him in order to keep his favour. He became so tired of his men saying, "O King, we know you are the most wonderful person in the world," or "O King, we know that there is nothing you cannot do," that he decided he would expose their foolishness. So he asked some of his servants to carry his throne down to the sea-shore.

Naturally, they wondered why the King had made such a strange request. They were even more curious as the King asked that his throne should be placed right at the water's edge. He sat down, facing out to sea.

Canute raised his arm, and looking out across the water, he shouted in solemn tones, "Stop! I command the sea to stand still immediately!" His courtiers looked on in amazement. Canute lowered is arm, and waited. Nothing happened. The waves behaved exactly as before, and the tide, which was coming in at the time, continued to do so. Canute's feet and legs would have been submerged if he had not requested his men to move his throne away from the water's edge when they saw what was happening.

"You see," said Canute, "Here is one thing I cannot do. I cannot stop the sea. There are many, many other things I cannot do; things that only God can do. So let me have no more of this stupid flattery!"

Naturally, all the King's courtiers felt very foolish for all the silly things they had said to Canute in the past.

Canute decided to hang his crown in a nearby Church to emphasise that he ruled over his people only because God willed it; and to show that God is the only One to whom nothing is impossible.

To think about:

Many people are seduced by the flattery of others, and begin to think that they are very wonderful in their own right. It takes a great man to turn away from the flattery of others, and to appreciate the motives that prompt people to utter false praise. Canute was such a man.

All those in positions of power or authority are liable to be flattered by those who would seek their favours. Only by a continual realisation of our utter dependence on God can we keep a sense of proportion in life. There is in every one of us the seed of conceit and self-importance. We have to learn to check these impulses.

Christ said, "Blessed are the meek for they shall inherit the earth." There are many people mentioned in the story of Jesus in the Gospels who were full of their own importance. Jesus often had words to say about those who observed every letter of the Law (and liked everyone to know that they were doing so, for it seemed that by doing this they thought they were entitled to be looked upon as self-righteous and important people), but who failed miserably to live up to the spirit of the Law.

A Prayer:

O Lord, help us to check the desire to be self-important in life. Show us that true greatness comes from serving others under Thee in true humility of spirit.

For further reading:

Gattey, C.N.   King Canute, the man who could not stay the tide.
and Moore, Z.B.   Epworth

ROY CASTLE

By any standards, Roy Castle is listed among the most versatile of recent entertainers. He had been known to play a tune on 40 different instruments, and in addition to his musical talent he sang, danced and made his audience laugh.

He was born near Huddersfield in 1932. His father was an insurance agent. Times were not easy, but the Castle household was a happy one. Mr and Mrs Castle senior were committed Christians, and Roy grew up in a Christian atmosphere.

He suffered from poor eyesight, and this proved to be a grave handicap at school. In fact, the trouble was not discovered until he had been to school for some time, and Roy then had a hard task to catch up with the others.

Everything possible was done by his parents to encourage Roy in his talents, and his parents brought him many things, including an expensive set of drums. At the age of 15 he decided to become a professional entertainer, and began at Clevelys summer show for £10 a week.

After a spell in the R.A.F. on national service, he passed through a hard time, with no employment, and then, when he was almost in despair, he received an offer to work as a partner with Norman Teal, a comedian he knew personally. Afterwards he worked with Jimmy Clitheroe at Blackpool in his summer show. Things were looking up. After touring with Jimmy Jones for some time, he was asked by Dickie Valentine to take part in his T.V. Show, and later a booking followed at the Prince of Wales Theatre. Since that time he became a firm favourite in the entertainment world, and appeared frequently in America and in this country. Several times he featured in Royal Variety shows.

In 1962 he was introduced by Eric Morecambe to a dancer in one of the shows, and a year later she and Roy were married. They had four children.

Roy's Christian upbringing stood him in good stead through his life, and although, like most people, he had doubts at various times of his life, he never lost his faith. He was a regular churchgoer, and often held a Bible study group in his own home.

Success goes to many people's heads, making them think they are self-sufficient, and can do without God, and without other people. But not so Roy; he retained his warmth of character, and also his sense of dependence on God. In spite of a very busy life, he always had time to think of those who were less fortunate than he was. He took an active interest in the Cheshire Homes, which do a great work for people suffering form serious diseases.

Sadly he died of cancer on 2nd September, 1994, but throughout his illness he looked forward eagerly to his future life with his Heavenly Father.

To think about:
It is very easy for people who reach the top in their career, and who become famous, to think that they can manage without anyone else, or indeed without God. But success never lasts for ever, and sooner or later the most successful person has to come to terms with the fact that he is a "has been". Success should never go to our head. We need God to give us support in our times of failure. We also need other people, and success should never make us feel we can do without them.

Do you know of any people who have made a name for themselves, and who, in their own sphere, are famous? Have these people lost their sense of proportion, i.e. has the fame gone to their heads? Or are they able to be normal people in their relationship with others in spite of their fame?

A Prayer:
O Lord, help us, we pray Thee, in all our times of need, when things seem black, and life is hard-going. And may we never lose sight of Thee when the going is good, and when we feel on top of the world. Teach us our need of Thee all the time, for Thy Name's sake.

For further reading:

| This is our Life. | Phil Mason | Published by the author at 1 Whitney Road, Burton Latimer, Kettering Northants. |

EDITH CAVELL

Edith, born in 1865, was the second daughter of the Vicar of Swardesdon, Norfolk, and his wife. When she was twenty two years old, she inherited some money and used it to travel to Central Europe. She was particularly impressed with Bavaria and its people, and she donated money towards a hospital there.

Her first job was as a governess in England, but later she moved to Belgium. She liked living in Brussels, and looking after children there.

In 1895 she returned home to see her father, who was in poor health, and at this time she decided to become a nurse. After a long period of training and service in England, including a few years as Superintendent of the Highgate Infirmary, she returned to Belgium in 1906, and here she was given the task of transforming a private clinic into a teaching hospital. She was widely acclaimed for this work. Each year she went home for a holiday, and while she was in Norfolk in 1914, World War I was declared. She rushed back to Belgium just as German troops invaded the country.

Although she could have escaped from the enemy, her sense of Christian duty gave her the will to stay at her post with other English nurses.

Eventually some wounded British soldiers came to the hospital for treatment, and after they had recuperated, Edith helped them to escape by a secret route to Holland, which was neutral. The soldiers eventually reached England, and for the next eight months Edith helped British, French and Belgian wounded soldiers escape into Holland. Some of the soldiers brought back with them intelligence about the position of German forces and equipment.

Edith realised that one day she would be arrested, and it was not long before the German authorities became suspicious. On August 5th, 1915, the hospital was raided and Edith was seized.

She freely admitted to the German authorities what she had been doing, and was sent to prison for ten weeks to await trial. During this time she was very calm and composed, spending her time in prayer and in reading religious books. Her composure greatly impressed her captors.

On 7th October, she was court-martialled, and she made no secret of what she had done. She probably expected at worst a period of hard labour, but four days later she learned she had been sentenced to be shot. She still remained remarkably calm.

Appeals were made by neutral diplomats for clemency, but Edith refused to beg for mercy. She was allowed to receive Holy Communion from an English padre in her cell, after which she said, "It is not enough just to be patriotic. I must have no hatred or bitterness towards anyone". Next morning she was shot by a firing squad.

A week later English newspapers heard the news, and Englishmen and women were furious. Edith was only forty nine years old when she died. Thousands of men volunteered for the army when they heard of the shooting of the nurse.

After the war, a special service was held in Westminster Abbey, and Edith's body was re-buried outside the walls of Norwich Cathedral. Not long afterwards a grey granite statue of her, forty feet high, was unveiled in London. Even today the shooting of Edith Cavell is looked upon with horror by many people, though it must be remembered that she was never in any sense a spy.

To think about:

The most remarkable thing about Edith Cavell was not her great patriotism. Thousands upon thousands of brave men and women, Christians and non-Christians alike, have supported their country in difficult times, in both war and peace, and have earned the title of patriot. Love of one's country springs from very deep roots, and is to be admired. But Edith Cavell displayed her Christian Spirit to the full when she looked into the faces of those who were about to take her life, and harboured no bitterness or hatred against them. To show forth feelings of love and kindness towards one's enemies, at a time when the outlook is bleak, is most decidedly a Christian virtue.

A Prayer:

O God, help us to face our difficulties and dangers in the spirit of Nurse Edith Cavell, and if ever we are called upon to suffer at the hands of an enemy, help us to look with love on those who seek to harm us. We ask this in the name of Jesus Christ, who suffered at the hands of His enemies, but who forgave, even on the Cross, those who wanted to destroy Him. Amen.

For further reading:

Heroes and Heroines	Antonia Fraser	Weidenfield & Nicholson 1979
Ready to Die	Peachment	Wheaton, 1979

LEONARD CHESHIRE

Leonard Cheshire was a bomber pilot in the Second World War, and he had some hair-raising escapes from death while flying over Germany. He was awarded the Distinguished Service Order for his flight back from Germany in a bomber which had been crippled while over enemy territory. By 1943 he was a Wing Commander, and had been awarded numerous other honours. He led the now-famous Dam Buster Squadron on forty raids, and eventually was able to calculate that he had completed a hundred "trips" over enemy territory – a rare achievement, because losses of planes and pilots were heavy. Now he was awarded the coveted Victoria Cross, the highest award for gallantry that the Armed Forces can give, bearing the two simple words, "For Valour".

In 1945, Cheshire went as an Observer with the American plane which was to drop one atom bomb on Nagasaki, in Japan. The searing flash and the horrifying explosion so sickened him that from that moment onwards his whole life changed, and he realised that when all the terrible fighting was over he must do something for the good of Mankind.

He first tried to form colonies of people in which each worked for the good of all; but these were a failure. Then he became a Roman Catholic, following the death of a dear friend of the same persuasion. Cheshire had admired the wonderful courage of his friend while he had nursed him through a terminal illness in a large house he had bought in Hampshire.

A deep love of his fellow-man prompted Cheshire to admit to this house a number of people suffering from incurable illnesses. No-one in need who knocked at the door was turned away. The success of this Home for Incurables led him to open others. The task he had set himself was a formidable one, and Cheshire worked himself so hard that he became seriously ill himself, and was confined to bed with tuberculosis for two years. While he was in bed he dreamed of other ideas to help his fellow-men. But of all the wonderful work done by this great Christian, he will be chiefly remembered for his great concern, not only in England but also in India, Malaya and Africa, for unfortunate human beings suffering from incurable diseases. The Cheshire Homes are a living testimony to a noble, selfless life.

In 1959 he married Sue Ryder, another remarkable soul, and she helped her husband in many of his ventures for sick people. She will always be remembered for her work with Stateless refugees after World War II. Many times she drove a lorry from England to Central Europe, and here she would pick up a load of the pitiful victims of Hitler's concentration camps, and bring them back to England to restore them to health.

Leonard Cheshire died in 1992, and his wife in the year 2000.

To think about:

Is there still a place in this country for homes and hospitals founded by private individuals, or ought the Government to do everything that is necessary? What differences might there be between a home run by the State? Some people think that small hospitals can offer the patient more personal attention than the big ones. What do you think?

A Prayer:

O God, bless all those who care for other people. Bless, too, all who are unhappy and insecure. Give to those who suffer from diseases which no doctor can cure the sure knowledge that they are in Your safe keeping.

For further reading:

Hughes, C.	Leonard Cheshire V.C. (Living Biography Series)	Phoenix
Braddon, Russell	Cheshire V.C.	Evans Cadet Editions
Unstead, R.J.	Great Leaders	A. & C. Black

FATHER DAMIEN

Leprosy is a terrible disease. The outward signs are horribly disfiguring. Large, open sores eat their way into the body, so that fingers, toes and nose drop off, and the whole body gradually wastes away. The patient dies a lingering death, too horrible to describe. Today, with new discoveries in medicine, there is a great deal of hope for the leper, but in days gone by there was little or none. Possibly the worst part of the disease was that many used to think it represented God's vengeance on an individual for some dreadful sin he had committed.

Lepers were usually separated from their fellow-men. In Biblical times they were often forbidden to come within the gates of a city, so kind people had to leave food outside the walls for them. Wherever they went, lepers had to shout, "Unclean! unclean!" to warn others, and sometimes they also had to ring a bell. Some people were so superstitious they thought they could catch leprosy if ever the shadow of a leper fell across them. In more recent times, lepers were often forced to live in isolation in colonies, and frequently they were left in these places all alone to fend for themselves without help. Such a colony existed on the island of Molokai, in the Hawaiian Islands, and it is here that our story is set.

Father Damien, a Belgian priest, was born in 1840, the son of a small farmer. His real name was Joseph de Veuster. In 1873, he felt it his Christian duty to go in place of his brother, who was ill, to minister to the wretched lepers of Molokai. Conditions on the island were even worse than he had feared. The six hundred lepers lived in hovels which were little better than pigsties. There was no sanitation or drainage for the dwellings. But the worst feature of all was that the lepers knew only too well that they were social outcasts, and this affected their behaviour to each other. Many behaved little better than beasts.

Damien told them about Jesus Christ, Who loved them and cared for their well-being. He had an uphill task in getting through with his message to these hardened souls. He helped to tackle their housing problems, and to lay on a proper water supply. He built a church, comforted the dying, and helped to dig graves. He bound up the lepers' wounds, and, in an effort to gain their confidence, he even shared his pipe with them – a step which he knew might easily prove fatal. Gradually, the attitude of the lepers changed from one of suspicion towards him to one of love.

One day, Damien spilled some boiling water on his foot and felt no pain. From that time onwards, he knew that he had leprosy himself, and he now addressed the congregation as, "We lepers".

He accepted his fate with joy, and died on 15th April 1889, aged only 49. His great work was done, but his example of self-sacrifice will live for ever.

To think over:

Would we give up a life of ease, without any hope of financial rewards, to help others who were distressed?

Would we leave friends and relatives for ever in order to help suffering Mankind?

Was Father Damien really happy with his lot, do you think, or did he just put on a brave show for the sake of the lepers?

A Prayer:

Lord, teach me that the easy way is not always the best way. Give me the courage to make right choices, even when there is danger present.

For further reading:

Mackinnon, Cleodie	Stories of Courage	Oxford Children's Reference Library No. 5 (page 60) O.U.P.
Farrow, J.	Damien the Leper (1937)	Burns, Oates and Co.

GRACE DARLING

Grace Darling's home was the Longstone Lighthouse, in the Farne Islands, off the Northumberland coast. Her father, William Darling was the lighthouse keeper. The sixty-three feet high tower had been Grace's home since she was ten years old. She often went to sleep to the sound of wild rain and howling wind beating on her window, and the huge waves breaking on the rocky base of the lighthouse.

One stormy night, on 6th September 1838, a particularly fierce gale was blowing. Terrific gusts of wind whipped up the waves into a wild fury, and towering breakers crashed with a thunderous roar on to the rocks. That night, unknown to Grace, the steamship Forfarshire, sailing from Hull to Dundee with sixty-one people on board, had run into serious trouble in the storm, and had been driven by the wind on to jagged rocks about a mile from the lighthouse. Nine people managed to scramble from the wreck, and to cling for their lives to the rocks.

Next morning, Grace was looking with the aid of her telescope across the wild sea, when she suddenly saw the wreckage and the people clinging to the rocks. She ran quickly to her father, and suggested a rescue operation immediately; but her father was of the opinion that with the sea in such a wild state their own little boat would be useless, unless he had another man with him.

"But I can go with you," pleaded Grace, who instinctively knew where her Christian duty lay. In spite of the protestations of her father and mother, she helped to launch the boat, and then set off in the tiny craft with her anxious father towards the stranded travellers.

After what seemed hours of toil, with the wind and rain lashing their faces, and with the lifeboat being tossed about by the foaming breakers, they came to the jagged rocks. Mr Darling sprang on to a slippery ledge, while Grace did all she could to hold the boat as securely as possible to save it from being torn open on the rocky fangs which protruded through the water. Only five of the soaked, frightened travellers could be rescued at the first attempt, and another perilous journey was necessary to rescue four more people.

Grace was not a strong girl, and this episode had sapped her strength. Four years later, she was dead. She had grown thin and weak, and tuberculosis had taken its toll. But the name of Grace Darling will never be forgotten wherever deeds of bravery and heroism are recalled.

To think over:

What made Grace face death in that dreadful storm? Was it just her compassion for those who were shipwrecked? Do you think she would have behaved like that if she had not been a Christian? If you think she would, did being a Christian make any difference at all? What should we do in a similar situation?

What do you know of the work of the Royal National Lifeboat Institution?

A Prayer:

Lord, give us the strength and courage to cope with any challenges with which we are confronted. Help us never to flinch from danger when it lies in the path of duty to God and to our fellow men.

For further reading:

Bigland, Eileen   The True Book about Heroines of the Sea

Frederick Muller

HENRY DUNANT

This great benefactor was born in May 8th, 1822, to a Swiss Christian businessman, who spent his spare time helping the poor. With this background, it was easy for Henry to follow the parental example and he became a member of a group of Christians committed to good works. His Christian group met with others in neighbouring countries and in 1855 a World Conference was held to discuss issues of common concern to the groups.

But young Henry had not yet found work to do, so his father pressed him to become a Bank Clerk. He was sent to one of the Bank's branches in Algeria, but his mind was still preoccupied with doing good Christian works. He purchased a farm and a mill, and tried to buy a tract of government land on which he could raise crops to feed the poor. But as Algeria belonged to France. Henry felt his best plan would be to contact the Emperor Napoleon (nephew of the famous Napoleon Bonaparte) regarding the purchase.

The Emperor was about to engage in battle in Italy against Austria, and could not thus spare the time to see Henry. But the young man did witness the fighting, the bloody Battle of Solferino, after which 40,000 men lay killed or injured on the battlefield. The suffering made a deep impression on Henry, and he gathered together groups of volunteers to nurse the wounded in a nearby Church. In doing this he saved many lives.

So horrified was he at the lack of medical care for wounded soldiers after a battle at that time that he wrote a book describing his experiences at Solferino. Consciences were stirred, and a great meeting was called at Geneva in 1863 to discuss how wounded soldiers could best be helped after a battle. Next year the recommendations of the meeting were embodied in a statement known as the Geneva Convention and many nations agreed to be bound by its regulations concerning the treatment of all wounded soldiers, friends or foes. The sign of the organisation which had been brought into being as the result of these meetings was to be a red cross on a white background. Thus the Red Cross Society was born. Later its activities were extended to include the investigation of Prisoner of War camps, and the sending of parcels to prisoners. Peacetime activities were to include earthquake, flood and famine relief.

Dunant strangely lapsed into obscurity after these important meetings, but he was rediscovered in 1895 by a newspaper reporter, and was awarded in 1901 the first Nobel Prize for Peace. He died in 1910 in Switzerland.

To think about:
Often large organisations grow from small beginnings. As David Everett wrote, "Tall oaks from little acorns grow." The Red Cross was one such organisation. A Christian, overcome by compassion at the sight of wounded men on a battlefield, decided that something must be done for these poor creatures. This was the beginning of what later became a huge international organisation, dedicated to the relief of suffering in many forms.

Many people would see in this wonderful story the outworking of the Holy Spirit of God through people dedicated to serving Him.

We just don't know what effect our actions, good or bad, may have in this world, as the repercussions of what we do spread outwards like ripples on the surface of a pond. This is surely food for thought.

A Prayer:
O Lord, help us to see that what we do does make a real difference. Guide us to make our world a better place by acts of love and kindness, that in so doing we may make a real contribution to the happiness of those around us.

For Further reading:
Peacey, Brenda   The Story of the Red Cross   Muller

ERIC

I do not know the full name of the person in this story. It is a tale of long ago, reported to be true.

Many years ago, before railways were common in Russia, a Baron and his family were driving by horse and carriage from the Russian frontier to St Petersburg. It was a bitterly cold day, with a sprinkling of snow on the ground, and the family were well wrapped up against the elements.

At sunset the carriage stopped at the inn of a frontier town called Robrin. The Baron ought to have put up for the night at the town, but he was in a hurry to be away, and ordered that his horses be changed quickly.

The innkeeper pointed out the dangers of a night-time journey. The road was bad, and hungry wolves were always on the prowl in the forest through which they must pass. But the Baron would not heed the advice of the inn keeper, merely stating that if he had four good horses he would reach Rostov before nine o'clock that night.

The first part of the journey lay across a windswept, treeless plain, and the biting wind cut into the horses as they pushed forward. Then the snow began to fall, and the forest loomed ahead. The trees formed an evergreen archway across the narrow road, and to the travellers it seemed like passing through a long dark tunnel.

Suddenly there came a long, mournful howl from the direction of the forest. Wolves were on the prowl. "Get a move on, driver", urged the Baron, but Eric the driver needed no second bidding. Although they travelled as fast as the horses could carry them, the dreaded howling of the wolves came nearer. The Baron guessed that the pack was a large one, and that the biting cold had maddened the animals.

As the Baron loaded his pistols, his little daughter began to cry. The wolves were gaining all the time. Now they could be dimly seen, and the Baron estimated that there were about two hundred of them, led by a huge, grey animal.

The Baron fired, and killed the leader. The pack fell back to eat his body. In the meantime Eric tied a large piece of wood to a stick, and trailed it behind the carriage. He knew that wolves are cautious animals, and probably wouldn't pass the wood. It served to check the onrush, but only for a time, and then they came on again.

One of the horses was now cut loose. It bolted into the forest, pursued by the wolves. But after they had eaten it, their pursuit of the carriage continued. The other leading horse was now cut loose, and it suffered the same fate.

The lights of Rostov were now only two miles ahead. The carriage hurtled on, but still the pack drew nearer.

Eric turned to the Baron. "There is only one hope in this situation", he said "I must keep the wolves at bay while you drive on for help. We just can't spare another horse."

"You will certainly die if you do," said the Baron, but by this time Eric had jumped from the carriage. The Baron fired into the pack; then the occupants of the coach heard two more shots, followed by a scream.

Still the wolves pressed on, and by now they were level with the carriage. The whole party yelled in unison at the tops of their voices, and this, together with the stream of light from the carriage window, checked the wolves so that Rostov was reached without further mishap.

No trace of Eric was ever found, apart from his pistol, but on the spot where he jumped from the carriage the Baron erected a stone cross, with the story of Eric's devotion engraved upon it.

To think about:

The history books are full of wonderful stories of bravery, and of men and women who gave their lives that others might live. Jesus said, "Greater love hath no man than this, that a man lay down his life for his friends" (John 15.13). We don't even know Eric's other name, but his story will never die.

A Prayer:

O God, we thank You for all the brave men and women who gave their lives so that others might live. We think especially of the sacrifice of our Lord Jesus Christ upon the Cross, so that we might all be forgiven for our wrong doing, and so that we might all inherit everlasting life. May we all be worthy of His great sacrifice. Amen.

For further reading:

Mighty men and Their Daring Deeds. Nathaniel Wiseman. Wesleyan Methodist Sunday School Union.

JOHN FLYNN

This great Australian was born in Victoria in 1880. He began his working life as a teacher, but after a few years he became a Minister of the Presbyterian Church.

He was given the task of preaching the Gospel to the white farmers and their aboriginal farmhands in the vast outback of Australia, where neighbouring farmers can be hundreds of miles apart, and where drought is an ever-present threat.

Flynn's journeys between the farms made him realise how difficult it was for those isolated people to obtain help in times of crisis, as when sudden illness struck. He therefore enlisted the help of the medical authorities, and arranged that nurses should be installed at strategic points over the vast area under his care, which covered about two million square miles. But the nurses proved unable to cope with the more serious illnesses, as they were working at great disadvantages. Somehow doctors had to be available quickly and means had to be found to transport sick people, where necessary, to hospital.

Two inventions of the day provided Flynn with the answer to his problems. Aeroplanes must be used to transport patients, and radio must be employed to send and receive news of sick people.

Initial radio experiments for John Flynn were made by George Towns, a radio enthusiast. He attempted to build suitable transmitters to send messages in Morse Code. Later a radio engineer names Alfred Traeger designed a two-way radio set, by means of which messages could be sent in speech instead of Morse Code. The power for the radio set was generated by turning two pedals with the feet, like riding a bicycle. This type of generator had been used earlier to provide electricity to work a cinematograph in Melbourne.

Many people worked with Flynn to build up the fine service which later became known as the Royal Flying Doctor Service. The first man to serve as a doctor in this venture was Dr. K St. Vincent Welch. Soon, doctors were regularly giving advice over the radio for the treatment of the less serious medical cases, and if the more serious cases warranted hospital treatment, the doctors would fly out to the farms and land on specially cleared strips. The patients, under the charge of the doctors, would then be flown to hospital. Many lives were saved in this way, and Flynn and his colleagues could truly be said to have brought a "mantle of safety" to the Outback settlers.

Later, the two-way radio system was also used for sending school lessons over the air to the children on lonely farms. Children could now discuss their problems with their teachers over the radio, and send in their lessons by post for marking.

John Flynn gave a lifetime of service to helping people who were cut off from civilisation. He died in 1951, and is buried near Alice Springs, in the heart of the great continent to which he dedicated his life. His work goes on.

To think over:

How would we cope with working in a very lonely place, hundreds of miles from civilisation?

What things would we miss the most? What would we most like to take with us from civilisation?

Would our faith stand the test of a hard life, with no comforts?

A Prayer:

O God, bless, we pray Thee, all lonely people. Help us never to feel cut-off, even in times of great loneliness, as long as we have You.

For further reading:

Brown, Barry	Flying Doctors	Lutterworth
Davey, Cyril	Fifty Lives for Christ	Oliphants

ELIZABETH FRY

Elizabeth Fry, born on 21st May 1780 at Gurney Court, Norwich, was the third daughter of a wealthy wool merchant and banker. The family belonged to the society of Friends, or Quakers, and each Sunday they worshipped at the Friends' Meeting House in Norwich. It was here, in 1797, that Elizabeth decided that she would dedicate her whole life to God through service to her fellow-men.

Taking a special interest in poor people, she began to visit their homes and teach their children. Even after she married Joseph Fry in 1800, and began to raise a family, she maintained her interest in the poor, nursing them and teaching their children as opportunity offered.

In 1813 she heard about the terrible plight of women prisoners in Newgate Gaol, in London. This was one of the many over-crowded prisons of the age. Laws were very savage in these days, and people could receive long sentences for small crimes. Prisons were dark and dirty, and many died of disease. Some were even chained in their cells. Women criminals had to take their children to prison with them, and nothing seemed to be done to teach criminals to be better citizens. Elizabeth was very moved by what she heard.

She managed to gain access to Newgate Prison, and asked to be allowed to go alone into a filthy room where many women were screaming and fighting. When she entered, the women were so shocked to see someone from outside, unprotected, in their midst, that they crowded round her and stared as if they were looking at a circus freak. Somehow, however, she managed to gain their confidence, and she picked up some of the children and nursed them.

In 1871 she formed an association for the improvement of the lot of women prisoners. She made frequent visits to Newgate, and became friends with many of the inmates. She gave them hope for the future, and told them about God. She often taught the children, and showed the women how to make and mend clothes.

Members of Parliament who had heard of her efforts came to visit the prisons, and afterwards, before a special House of Commons Committee, Elizabeth was thanked for her great work. She showed influential people that prisons should not be places just for punishment, but that the prisoners, if treated wisely, could be reformed, so that they could make a new start.

Many other prisoners, not only in England but also in several European countries, were visited by her. She continued to befriend the poor in every way she could, for she felt that many of them had not had a fair start in life. In 1817 she founded an association to supply clothes to the destitute, and three years later she helped to form a nightly shelter for the London Homeless. Throughout her life she felt that God was guiding her in all that she did.

She died at Ramsgate on 12th October 1845, after a very busy life. She had several children.

To think over:
Do we tend to look upon those who go to prison with a rather superior air, thinking ourselves to be better than they are? Or do we honestly believe that "there, but for the Grace of God, go I"? What do we think that imprisonment should do for the prisoner? Should it just punish and deter people from doing the same things again? Or should it, in addition, try to make better citizens of the prisoners? Are sentences today severe enough? Should those who murder someone be killed themselves? Many people today think that prison life is too "soft". Find out what you can about prison life, and see what you think about this.

A Prayer:
In spite of the attractions of some of the things we know to be wrong, help us, O God, to go through life in the way we know to be right. Help us always to look for ways of serving our fellow-men, and never to let our greed get the better of us.

For further reading:
Northcott, C.   Angel of the Prisons   Lutterworth

DUDLEY GARDINER

Dudley Gardiner was born in England in 1910. He had many of the shortcomings of a boisterous young man of his day – he was often aggressive and destructive in outlook. What better outlet for such a young man than a life in the army? So Dudley enlisted as a boy soldier.

During the Second World War, he served with the British Forces in Burma, fighting the Japanese, who are among the most tenacious of enemies. Here he was taken prisoner, and he suffered terrible hardships in captivity. But adversity often makes people reassess their values, and so it was with Dudley. While a prisoner of war he had plenty of time to think about the real purpose of life, and for him this was a turning point.

He decided to retire early, and to spend the remainder of his life helping less fortunate human beings. He went to Geneva and Hong Kong to look for a fulfilling role, but finding nothing to suit him, he moved to Calcutta, which he had visited while on military service.

The more he investigated the living conditions of the poor in this city of nearly nine million people, the more horrified he became. Many thousands had no work, and nearly three quarters of a million people had no proper home. They slept on the pavements or on the rooftops. Some built flimsy shacks from cardboard and corrugated iron sheets.

Floods played havoc with these temporary hovels, and disease was rampant in the overcrowded conditions. Many were unable to buy even the barest necessities of life, and lived in a state of starvation. Deaths were common.

Dudley Gardiner's heart was touched. Gathering together all the help he could, he joined forces with the Salvation Army Social Services team in Calcutta, to start a daily feeding programme for 5,000 people at the Social Services Centre. He spent about five hours a day taking milk and food round to the poorest families in the slums. A rota of social workers was organised to visit poor people, and to give out free meal tickets where appropriate.

Every day for twenty years Dudley took a leading part in the feeding of the underprivileged masses in this great city. The food was given for the most part by generous organisations in Europe and America, but the preparation of the meals was in itself a major task each day. Dudley had his own personal health problems – he suffered from a condition called elephantiasis which caused his legs to swell – but this did not deter him from what he knew to be his Christian duty. No wonder he was known as "The Angel with the Bushy Beard". He received the M.B.E. for his services, but would not miss his rounds even to receive this. He gave his army pension towards the work to which he had dedicated his life.

Dudley Gardiner died in May, 1981, aged 71 years.

To think about:

There are still millions of starving people in the world today, though there is food enough to feed them if it could all be distributed where it was needed. The trouble is that the world's poverty occurs in those countries which just cannot afford to pay for all the food they need. Fortunately, many well-meaning people from Europe and North America dedicate years of their lives to working among these unfortunate people, to feeding them, and to making them as healthy as they can. But thousands upon thousands still starve to death. The problems of rich nations and poor nations existing side by side on earth is one of the major difficulties of today's world, and no-one has yet found the answer to it.

A Prayer:

O God, help us always to realise that there are millions of men and women, boys and girls, in the underdeveloped countries living in conditions of indescribable filth and squalor. Make us always mindful of our Christian duty to love one another, and show us how we can be of service in our lives to those who are hungry or in poor health. We ask this in the name of Your Son, our Saviour, Jesus Christ. Amen.

For further reading:

The Salvation Army, 101 Newington Causeway, London SE1 6BN has information on Dudley Gardiner

THOMAS GUY

Thomas Guy, born in Horsleydown, Southwark, in 1645, the son of a lighterman, was a hard old skinflint. Everyone knew that. He lived in London at the time of the Great Plague. Large numbers of people died, their corpses being piled on to carts which creaked along cobbled streets at dead of night as the driver called out, "Bring out your dead!"

Guy was apprenticed to a Bookseller named John Clarke, who had a shop in Cheapside, but later he set up in business for himself. The business flourished, and he became rich. He made a feature of selling smuggled cheap imported Bibles in his shop, at a time when Bibles were not allowed to be brought into this country. From 1679 to 1692 he was the printer to Oxford University.

In spite of his wealth, he dressed very plainly, and never spent any money on luxuries, as did his business acquaintances. He hated banquets and festivities, and because of this he turned down an offer to become Sheriff of The City of London, though he did serve as M.P. for Tamworth for a time.

Many stories, some no doubt apocryphal, were told about him. According to one of these, he would often be seen sitting in his shabby shop at meal-times, chewing a crust of dry bread. Such was his appearance that on one occasion, according to another story, he was leaning on the parapet of London Bridge, lost in thought, when a stranger offered him money, thinking he was a down-and-out about to commit suicide.

A third tale tells how, one evening, a business acquaintance came to talk to him in an attempt to discover the secret of how he made his wealth. Guy suggested that they talk in the dark, to save the cost of the candle-light! No wonder the local boys thought him a figure of fun, for they would shout insults after him as he walked along the streets.

Guy made a number of very shrewd business investments, especially in the South Seas Company, and he sold his stock at the most advantageous time, making huge profits. No-one had the vaguest notion of what he did with the money. Few knew that one of his main interests was the local hospital. Only a small number of his closest associates realised that when three new wards were added to the hospital in 1707, they were a gift from Thomas Guy. Even fewer people knew that Guy had been responsible for giving pensions to many poor widows in the City.

In 1722, when Guy was seventy-seven people noticed a great new hospital being built near St. Thomas's, but again they did not connect it with the man they often called the "miser". Guy had seen so many patients discharged from St. Thomas's as incurable that he was building another hospital to accommodate them. It became known as Guy's Hospital, and its founder left for its endowment more than £200,000.

Just when the new building was finished, Guy died (27 December 1724), and his Will was published. Many thousands of pounds were left to provide for the poor and the sick, not only in London, but also in Tamworth, the home of his mother. Guy had denied himself throughout his life in order to give his wealth to his less-fortunate fellow-men.

To think over:

If we had more money than we needed, should we keep it for ourselves, or should we give it away? If we decided to give it away, should we first of all think of our friends, who might one day do us a good turn in return, or should we first think of the needy, at home and overseas, who could never repay us in kind?

Is it morally wrong to make a lot of money?

Find out all you can about Lord Nuffield, and of how he helped suffering humanity with the money that he made in the motor-car industry.

A Prayer:

O Lord, teach me always to be generous in thought, in word, and in deed. Help me always to think more of other people than I do of myself, for Your dear sake.

For further reading:

For biographical details, consult the Dictionary of National Biography.

Cameron, H.C.   Mr Guy's Hospital, 1726-1948   Longmans Green 1954

ROBERT STEPHEN HAWKER

Jesus never said that to follow Him meant taking life very seriously at all times. Indeed, a happy disposition is a great asset to a Christian. Some followers of Jesus Christ have been characters noted for their wit and even for their eccentricity, though deep inside their personalities they have retained a profound concern for the things in life which really matter. One of the most amusing of eccentric Christians was Robert Stephen Hawker, who became Vicar of Morwenstow, Cornwall.

He was born in Devon on December 3rd, 1804, and was educated at Cheltenham Grammar School and Pembroke College, Oxford. At the age of 21 he married a lady twenty years his senior. On his holidays from Oxford, he loved to sit on the Cornish cliffs overlooking the sea, and write poetry. One of his best-known pieces, called the Song of the Western Men, relates to the imprisonment of Bishop Trelawney of Bristol in 1688 by James II, and incorporates lines in use at that time:

And have they fixed the where and when?
And shall Trelawney die?
Here's twenty thousand Cornishmen
Will know the reason why!

Hawker was a flamboyant character, and many stories about him are told. One story, no doubt embellished with the passage of time, relates how at full moon in July, 1825, he sat on a rock in the sea off the coast of Bude in Cornwall, draped seaweed over his head to look like long hair, wrapped his legs in oilskins, and, naked to the waist, posed as a mermaid! He wailed and sang until a crowd gathered on the shore. After several nights of this he grew somewhat tired of his prank, gave a rendering of the National Anthem, and dived into the waves. The "mermaid" was never seen again!

In 1829 he became a Curate in North Tamerton. Wherever he went he took with him his pet pig on a lead, a big black animal called Gyp, who, faultlessly groomed and with impeccable manners, went visiting with Hawker into people's houses.

But there was another side to this remarkable man. These were the days of sailing ships, and there were frequent shipwrecks off the Cornish coast. At such times, Hawker, who was now Vicar of Morwenstow, would often risk his life to rescue unfortunate sailors and passengers. He would take the shipwrecked people back to his vicarage, attend to their needs, and give them presents when they departed. Those who died would be given a Christian burial.

He visited the poor in his parish regularly, took them gifts, and championed their cause in every way possible. His parishioners loved him, in spite of his odd ways. His worn clothing was of no concern to him; all his suits were threadbare.

Though he had some serious faults, including that of intolerance, he made a remarkable impact in his village. After his wife died he became very unhappy, and died in 1875.

We all have reason to be grateful to Robert Stephen Hawker, for to him we owe the revival of the Harvest Festival Service in our churches, including the blessing of the fruits of the earth. His grandfather, also a clergyman, wrote the well known school hymn, "Lord, dismiss us with Thy blessing".

To think about:
The world loves colourful characters like Hawker. Many of our best comedians and comics have been devout Christians. Do you know any "characters"? Do they have another side to their make-up, other than the one the world readily recognises? Is it wise to assess the real worth of people before we get to know them really well?

A Prayer:
O God, we thank You for the "characters" of this world, who add colour and variety of life. Help us never to judge people by their outward appearances, but to look beneath the surface for their real value. Amen.

For further reading:
References to Robert Stephen Hawker may be found in many Cornish guide books and Country books.

The Life and Letters of R.S. Hawker   C.E. Byles   1905

OCTAVIA HILL

Octavia Hill was born at Wisbech in Cambridgeshire, in 1838. Her father, a Banker, was noted for his good works. From the time she was a young girl, Octavia showed a great affection for other people. When she was fourteen she began work with an association formed by the Christian Socialists, of which Charles Kingsley, author of The Water Babies, was a prominent member. Later she started a school in London, and about this time became concerned about the housing conditions of the very poor people in London. She was appalled to see the overcrowded conditions, the dilapidated state of much of the rented property, and the filth and squalor in which many people lived. Many thousands of families lived in single-roomed accommodation.

She believed that much could be done to improve matters. With money raised by friends she bought houses, and began to put into practice some of her ideas as to how property management should be done. She attended to repairs promptly, avoided overcrowding, arranged her tenants so that neighbours were compatible with each other, and always approached her tenants with respect, in a way which showed she understood their problems.

In 1884 the Church Commissioners had faith enough in her methods to ask her to manage much of their property in the Southwark area of London.

So successful were her ideas that people from overseas, including America, copied her principles of house management.

But Octavia Hill's chief claim to fame is for something quite different from housing. She was a great champion of the need for preserving places of natural beauty, and places of historic interest, for the pleasure of ordinary people. With other like-minded people, she founded in 1895, the National Trust, an organisation which now owns and controls for the use of the public many beauty spots and places of historic interest. More and more areas of outstanding natural beauty are continually being given to the National Trust, which assumes the role of preserver of all that is good in the English countryside.

Octavia Hill believed profoundly in the great value of voluntary work, as compared with work done for a State organisation. She thought that voluntary work preserved the human touch. People did the work for the love and joy of doing it, not because it was just a job of work to be done.

She took the inspiration for her work from her profound Christian faith, and when she died in London, on August 13th, 1912, she left behind her a wonderful record of caring for souls who were less fortunate than she was, and a record of concern for the preservation of the countryside.

To think about:
We think of Octavia Hill and her work whenever we think of bad housing conditions, or of the preservation of the countryside. What a wonderful legacy she gave to posterity! Yet in all that she did she believed in voluntary organisations. Is there anything fundamental, do you think, which distinguishes a worker for a voluntary organisation, often grossly underpaid, from a person who works for a State organisation connected with welfare?
Make a list of the voluntary organisations in our country today that exist to save and to protect the underprivileged sections of our Society.

A Prayer
Lord, we thank You for the life of service to her fellow men and women of Octavia Hill. May we think of her when we see the beauty of Your unspoilt countryside, which she did so much to preserve. Help us, too, to lead dedicated lives like hers.

For further reading:

Hill, William Thomson   Octavia Hill,   Hutchinson
                         Pioneer of the National Trust
                         and Housing Reformer

TREVOR HUDDLESTON

Most of the part of Africa populated by black people has emerged from Colonial rule to independence in the second half of the twentieth century. Not that this has always been for the benefit of all black people. Sometimes black tyrants have seized power and have ruled ruthlessly, and the British concept of democracy has not evolved in most states. But it is interesting to see that some of the States have well-respected black Christian leaders, who have made important strides on the way to freedom and justice for their people.

South Africa had always been a most difficult problem. Here, the black people outnumber the whites many times, and in order to preserve the white identity the South African white people initiated the policy of "Separate Development" or Apartheid. Black people were allocated certain areas where they could rule themselves, but the white economy was entirely dependent on cheap black labour. Black workpeople who worked in white areas had to carry Passes, giving details of themselves, and white Police could demand to see the Passes at any time. The black people naturally resented this treatment, and sometimes tempers erupted when they felt that they were being treated as second-class citizens. At times the white Police had to fire at the blacks to quell the rioting, and there were many deaths.

In the white areas of South Africa, the blacks were segregated as much as possible. Seats in public transport were similarly segregated. Intermarriage between black and white races was forbidden.

It was this situation that so disturbed Trevor Huddleston when he first went to South Africa as a priest. Born in Bedford on 15th June, 1913, and educated at Oxford University, Trevor first travelled to the Far East, where he saw conditions of indescribable poverty and squalor. He returned to this country and trained to be a priest. As a curate in Swindon, he decided to join a monastic order at Mirfield in Yorkshire.

He was sent by the Monastery to take charge of a school and church in Sophiatown, a suburb of Johannesburg, in South Africa. Here he saw Apartheid in action, and he hated it from the start. He witnessed many injustices, and often tried to take the part of the blacks in confrontations with the Police. He started schemes to feed black children who were undernourished. Clubs for young blacks were begun. But he knew he was only scratching the surface of a tremendous problem.

The Police kept watch on him, and he was nearly imprisoned. Then he was called back to England, where his stand against tyranny had become known, and he was widely acclaimed for his work. By writing and broadcasting he was able to make Britain understand what was happening in South Africa.

Later he was appointed Bishop of Masai In Tanganyika, and eight years afterwards became Bishop of Stepney. In both these offices he tried to improve the lot of the poor and underprivileged. In 1978 he became Bishop of Mauritius, where he continued his fight for justice.

Father Huddleston died on 20th April, 1998 but in recent years democratic ideas have taken control in South Africa.

To think about:

All men are equal in the sight of God. This belief is fundamental to Christianity. People who cannot agree with this cannot possibly call themselves Christians. It is foolish to deny that many problems arise when people of different races try to live harmoniously side by side. Customs and cultures are different, and these differences often breed suspicion. The temperaments of people of different races is often a cause of friction. But everyone, no matter what the colour of his or her skin, is unique, and of infinite worth to his or her Maker.

Try to find out all you can about the problems of people of different cultures and races trying to settle in this country. Find out, too, all you can about the men and women of all races who are doing their utmost to bring the races together in harmony.

A Prayer:

O Lord, help us always to realise that You made all men equal in Your sight. Teach us to see that different races have different gifts to contribute, but that together we make up Your wonderful family of Mankind.

For further reading:

Huddleston, Trevor   Naught for Your Comfort   Collins/Fontana

EGLANTYNE JEBB

Eglantyne Jebb was born in 1876 of well-to-do parents in a large Shropshire manor house. After studying History at Oxford University, she was in a position to return to a life of leisure at home, but she was already firmly resolved as to the future course of her life. She was determined to work for children. For a time she was a teacher, but she found that this was not her real vocation, and she thought again about how she could do what she wanted to do.

Early in the twentieth century, following fighting in Greece, reports were received of many thousands of children who were in a desperate plight. Help was sent from Britain, and Eglantyne went out as a representative of the fund-raising body to see for herself the awful conditions of the children. Now she knew exactly where her life's work lay. Suffering children must be her special concern.

After the First World War there was enormous suffering in Europe, with millions of children hungry or diseased. Eglantyne started to raise money for a special fund to help these children, and in April, 1919, the now-famous Save the Children Fund came into being. The first contribution to the Fund was given by Miss Jebb's housekeeper.

However money, food and medical supplies were just not enough. Doctors and nurses were required, too. So the Organisation grew and grew until today it sends help into more than forty countries in various parts of the world.

Eglantyne travelled extensively, looking for areas where help with children was desperately needed. She met the leaders of many countries, and told them not just about suffering children in the world, but also about the fundamental principles she felt to be the birthright of all children. These included the right of a child to a healthy material, moral and spiritual development; the sanctity of the family unit; and an acknowledgement that race, nationality and creed were of no consequence in determining the child's rights.

With these and other ideals in her mind, Eglantyne Jebb formulated a "Charter of Children's Rights" in 1924, and these same principles were adopted by the League of Nations, and later, by the United Nations.

In spite of illness, this great lady continued to search throughout the world for areas of child deprivation. The activities of the Save the Children Fund are now known everywhere. She died in 1928, but left behind her a wonderful legacy of care and concern for the world's children. She always drew inspiration and strength from her Christian background.

To think about:

Eglantyne Jebb lived a life dominated by a consuming passion. She identified an area of real need in the world, and set about doing something about it with all her vigour. She left behind her a wonderful organisation which continues to do desperately needed work.

What causes are there in the world today which serve humanity, to which individuals can give themselves with dedication? There are many. There are still wars, poverty, famine, earthquakes and floods, as there always have been. Make a list of the organisations which help unfortunate people, and find out what you can about them.

A Prayer:

O Lord, give us the single-mindedness of purpose of Eglantyne Jebb. Help us to see where we can serve our fellow human beings, in the knowledge that in serving others we are serving Thee. For Your dear sake.

For further reading:

R.G. Martin   Save the Children   Lutterworth
Literature from Save the Children Fund, 17 Grove Lane, Camberwell, London SE5 8RD

EDWARD JENNER

Smallpox is an infectious disease which has been responsible for the deaths of literally millions of people. It was a Gloucestershire doctor who, at the end of the eighteenth century, found the answer to this scourge of Mankind.

Edward Jenner was born on May 17th, 1749, to the Rev. Stephen Jenner, Vicar of Berkeley, Gloucestershire, and his wife. He was the youngest of ten children, and both parents died when the boy was five. He went to live with one of his older brothers, who by this time was Rector of nearby Rockhampton.

After completing his education, at Wotton-under-Edge and later at Cirencester Grammar School, Edward began work as an assistant to a surgeon in one of the nearby towns, but later, when he was 21, he went to London to undertake medical studies under John Hunter, a great surgeon of the day. While in London he helped Sir Joseph Banks to arrange the zoological specimens which Banks had collected on Captain Cook's voyage of 1771.

Eventually, he became a surgeon in his own right, and returned to Gloucestershire to practise as a doctor and surgeon.

Jenner had for some time noticed that dairymaids who were in frequent contact with cows very often did not catch smallpox. Cows suffered from a milder disease called cowpox, and Jenner argued that if these milkmaids had in fact caught cowpox, this might have given them immunity to smallpox. If this was so, then it ought to be possible to vaccinate people against smallpox by giving them the germs of cowpox. There was some confusion in early experiments because there were two different diseases known as cowpox, but, as later tests showed, only one of the diseases gave people immunity from smallpox.

The first vaccination against smallpox was given by Jenner to a young boy on 14th May 1796.

While these experiments were in progress, Jenner had married Catherine Kingscote. Like her husband, Catherine was a Christian and she ran a number of Sunday Schools.

After the first successful vaccination against smallpox, Jenner spent all his spare time in spreading the news of his discovery, and in standardising vaccination procedure. He later suffered two strokes, the latter proving fatal, and he was found dead on 26th January, 1823. He was buried in Berkeley churchyard.

In addition to being a wonderful doctor and surgeon, Jenner was also a naturalist, and he made a number of important discoveries in this realm.

Edward Jenner will always be remembered for his remarkable work to rid mankind of one of its deadliest enemies.

To think about:
Try to find out all you can about diseases which have been largely eradicated, because of the wonderful work of doctors. Read about Sir Ronald Ross and his fight against malaria, another scourge; and about Jonas Salk and his fight against poliomyelitis. Read also about Alexander Fleming, who discovered by accident the greatest germ-killer of all time, penicillin.

Jenner was a Christian. Not all doctors are Christians. How does being a Christian help a doctor? What does Christ have to say about the great value of the individual human life? Read Matthew 10:29-31.

Some doctors think they should have the right to end life when a patient is suffering greatly with no hope of recovery. Other doctors think that to destroy life is wrong under any circumstances. What do you think?

A Prayer
O Lord, we thank you for the doctors and nurses, who have fought to rid Mankind of disease. Give them patience and understanding, and above all, reverence for human life. We ask this, knowing it is Thy Will.

For further reading
Rains, A.J.H.   Edward Jenner & Vaccination   Priory Press

HELEN KELLER

Helen Keller can surely be numbered with the most remarkable women who ever lived. She was born in 1880 in the U.S.A. and lived a normal life until she was eighteen months old. Then she suffered from an illness which left her blind, deaf and dumb. Medical attention was of no avail.

As she grew older, she learned by touching other people's faces that they were somehow communicating, but she had of course no understanding of what was actually happening. So she became very frustrated, and lapsed into violent tempers.

A marvellous teacher named Anne Sullivan was found for her. At first, there was little contact between the two, but after Anne had persisted in letting Helen see that she was going to do as she was told, and that she was not going to give in to the temper tantrums, the two gradually established a friendly relationship. Eventually by skilful teaching, a few words made by tapping the hand passed between them, and Anne realised that Helen was an intelligent girl. She was capable of accomplishing much more.

So she taught her to read Braille, a system in which the fingers are trained to recognise groups of dots in various patterns on paper, each pattern representing a letter. Later, Helen learned to type.

Now she set her mind to learning to speak. She placed her hands on her teacher's face and throat, and so sensitive were her fingers that she could distinguish minute differences in movement, and she tried to make sounds herself by imitating the throat and facial movements exactly.

She read the Bible in Braille, and so came to learn about God, and about Jesus Christ.

Later she left home for school, and her knowledge of the outside world grew and grew. She even learnt some foreign languages, and also to swim. When she knew a locality well she could go for a walk unaided.

She could assess people who were strangers to her by feeling their faces and their hands as they conversed. She even learned to understand what they were saying by touching their lips. She could pick up in her body the vibrations of people's footsteps, and identify people by this means.

As a devout Christian, Helen decided to travel overseas, and to work for blind people everywhere. She died in 1967, but left behind her a wonderful record of a brave woman who just would not admit defeat, and who tried to bring joy and gladness to others who were afflicted with blindness.

To think about:

There is no human story more wonderful than that of Helen Keller. She triumphed over afflictions which would have beaten thousands of others. She had a spirit that just would not admit defeat. What an example is her story to future generations! What a message of hope it carries! It is truly Christian to be able to face adversities with courage, secure in the knowledge that Jesus Christ is there to help us. Do you know of others who have courageously faced serious illness? There are probably one or two such people in your own street. Can non-Christians face suffering and pain in the same way as Christians? If so, what distinguishes the Christian from the non-Christian in this situation? Is it the hope with which a true Christian sufferer faces the future?

A Prayer:

Lord Jesus, we pray for all those who are deaf or blind or dumb. We think especially of those who face their condition with trust in the future; but we ask Your blessing on those who have no hope, and who need Your Divine help.

For further reading:

Tibble, J.W. & A.	Helen Keller	A. & C. Black
Evans, I.O.	Benefactors of the World	Warne
Pringle, P.	When they were Girls	Harrap

MARTIN LUTHER KING

Martin Luther King lived in Montgomery, Alabama, U.S.A. He was called to the Ministry of the Church at the age of seventeen; was trained at the Crozier Theological Seminary; and was appointed the negro Minister of the Baptist Church in Montgomery in 1954.

Montgomery is a town with a large black and white population, and, as in other parts of the southern United States, there is often racial tension. The black people are the descendants of slaves, and many white people there cannot accept fully the idea that God made all men, black and white, equal. Negroes still do not have the same treatment as white people in many areas.

Passions between black and white people never became more acute than they did one day in 1955, when a negro woman was asked to get up from her seat in a crowded bus to make way for a white man. She refused, was brought to court for disobeying the conductor, and was fined. This so incensed the negroes that they refused to travel on Montgomery buses until equal treatment was accorded to them. Martin Luther King, as the leader of the Negroes, told his people not to resort to violence or revenge in retaliation for what had been done.

The Supreme Court in Washington ruled that negroes were, under the Constitution of the United States, equal with whites in every respect, and the negroes knew that they had the law on their side. King warned them not to brag or boast about this, because it would only provoke violence. He believed that a cause could be won by making things difficult for those who are against one, without fighting or harming people. He organised many peaceful demonstrations to bring to the notice of all that negroes wanted their full rights as citizens. Unfortunately, he couldn't stop all the violence, but many white people as well as black came to his support. In 1963, as the culmination of a great Civil Rights march in Washington, King addressed a great rally, and he said that he dreamed one day that all men would live in harmony as equals.

King's work for peace was so great that in 1964 he was awarded the Nobel Peace Prize. He wrote several books supporting the cause of equality for coloured peoples. Some of the racial barriers are now beginning to break down in America, and negroes in many states of the U.S.A. are treated somewhat better than they were. But there is still a long way to go.

Many of those who supported the black people were attacked, and some were killed. King's turn came in 1967, when a white fanatic shot him dead. He was only 38 years old, but was not afraid to die. The great work he started goes on, but hatred still lingers in the hearts of many who do not agree with equal rights for coloured people. King's mother was tragically shot dead in 1974 while attending a church service.

To think about

Racial intolerance has been practised in many lands, including our own, throughout the history of Mankind. Find out what you can about the Ku Klux Klan, the secret American organisation dedicated to maintaining white supremacy.

Many people think that black people are inferior to white people in intellectual capacity, and that consequently they ought to be treated differently. Others think it is wrong to compare the two, because they have both inherited different cultures, and consequently have developed in different ways. Read what you can on this subject. Ought black and white people to live side by side, and send their children to the same schools? Are there any difficulties about this? Is peaceful resistance of any use as a means of solving social problems like racial intolerance?

A Prayer

O Lord, we know that all men are made in Your likeness. Help us to love them all as brothers.

For further reading

Preston, Edward	Martin Luther King: Fighter for Freedom	Doubleday
Slack, Kenneth	Martin Luther King	Allenson

MAKSYMILIAN KOLBE

In June, 1979, Pope John Paul II visited his native Poland. One of the places where huge crowds gathered was the World War II concentration camp at Oswiecim, or as the Germans called it, Auschwitz. Five million men, women and children were killed here by the Nazis. Among the former inmates of this dreadful place was a man named Franciszek Gajowniczek. At the time of the Pope's visit, Franciszek was 78 years old, and he had been saved from death in the camp by an extraordinary Polish priest, who is still greatly revered in his own country. His name was Maksymilian Kolbe.

He was born as Raymond Kolbe on 7th January 1894, and was one of five boys. Taught by his parents to read and write, Raymond later went to a monastery in Lwow, where he took a new name, Maksymilian. Much of his later study was done in Rome.

In spite of the discovery that he was suffering from tuberculosis, he persisted in his studies, and after gaining Doctorates of Philosophy and Theology, he was ordained a priest on 28th April, 1918. He then returned to Poland, but was forced to spend some time in a sanatorium. A saintly man, Father Kolbe was seized with a desire to bring the whole world to Christ, and he began to publish a religious magazine which gained a large circulation. Later he went as a missionary to Japan, but continued to suffer from bouts of severe illness. He returned to his native land in 1936.

Father Kolbe had a premonition when he was a boy that he would die a martyr's death, and he also had a very strong feeling that war was surely coming again, as indeed it did in 1939. Poland was in a very vulnerable position, lying between Germany and Russia, and as soon as hostilities broke out the Germans invaded Poland, rounding up all the key people as they did so. The took Father Kolbe prisoner, and led him away to a camp at Amtitz, and later to a dreaded prison at Pawiak, where he was tortured and taunted about his religion. In spite of being brutally beaten and starved, he prayed for his enemies and accepted the treatment he received with undisguised joy. Later he was moved to Auschwitz camp, a name that struck terror into the hearts of millions, because of the gas extermination chambers that the Nazis operated there.

One day, a prisoner escaped from the camp, and the Nazis decreed that twenty prisoners should die if he were not found. The man did not appear, so one of the German Officials selected at random from a row of men the twenty who were to be starved to death in the notorious Block Fourteen. Franciszek Gajowniczek was one of those chosen, but he cried out for mercy, as he had a wife and young children to look after. So, without hesitation, Father Kolbe, to the amazement of the German guards, stepped forward and offered to take the man's place.

In Block Fourteen the twenty people were ordered to strip, and were slowly starved to death over a period of days. The Polish corpse-bearer, who had to enter the death chamber every day to carry out the dead, reported later that Father Kolbe continued to pray all the time for his captors and for his fellow-prisoners. So died a brave, saintly priest of the Christian Church.

To think about

When Jesus was dying on the Cross, He said, "Father, forgive them, for they know not what they do". When Stephen, the first Christian martyr, was being stoned to death for his forthright preaching about Jesus Christ, he said, (doubtless remembering the words of Jesus) "Lord, lay not this sin to their charge". What wonderful acts of forgiveness! Could we ever forgive those who had done a dreadful wrong to us? Thousands of men and women have been killed in history for their belief in Jesus Christ, and there are many records of these Christians dying joyfully in these circumstances.

A Prayer

O Lord, Help us to forgive those who have done wrong to us, in the same way that, in the Lord's Prayer, we ask You to forgive us when we have done wrong to You.

For further reading:

Winowska, Maria   Our Lady's Fool   Mercia Press Ltd, Cork

JOSEPH LISTER

Lord Joseph Lister was one of the greatest English surgeons, and he is chiefly remembered for his work in making surgical operations safer.

Born at Upton, Essex, on 5th April 1827, he was one of seven children of a Quaker family. Quakers, sometimes known as the Society of Friends, always have a great sense of social responsibility, and a great respect for education and learning. Lister's father was famous for a compound microscope and a special type of lens which he had perfected. Young Joseph, even as a boy, made up his mind to become a doctor.

He went from school to University College, London, where he spent nine years training to be a surgeon. In 1846, at the age of 19, he witnessed the first operation performed in England with the use of anaesthetics. Before that time operations were performed on patients who had been rendered semi-conscious with alcohol, and several men had to hold them down by force while surgery was performed. Quite apart from the excruciating pain of the operation, the wounds of many of the patients became infected, because little was known about germs and infection.

Lister studied the problems of infected wounds, and read of the investigations of the Frenchman Louis Pasteur into the fields of fermentation and putrefaction. He began to realise that the formation of pus was due to bacteria, and he concentrated his efforts on the means of destroying them before they entered the body. There were three possible ways of doing this, by filtration, by heat or by chemicals, and Lister saw the latter as having the greatest promise. After numerous experiments, he selected carbolic acid as being the most suitable and powerful germicide for his purpose; and all his surgical instruments, dressings and wounds were treated liberally with this. Lister's first operation using carbolic acid was on a boy who had broken his leg when he was run-over by a cart. The sharp ends of the bone had pierced the skin, and these wounds might easily have turned septic, but fortunately, under Lister's skilled direction they did not.

The results of using carbolic acid as a disinfectant were dramatic. Deaths from infection went down immediately, in spite of the fact that the acid Lister used at first was found to be far too concentrated, and tended to burn the skin and the wounds. It was later made much safer by using weaker solutions.

Our modern operating theatres owe much to Lister's discovery. One of the greatest qualities of the man was that in spite of his becoming very famous, he was always very gentle and unassuming in his manner. Honours were showered upon him for his work. He was created Baronet in 1883, and in 1902 was awarded the Order of Merit. He died on 10th February 1912.

To think about

How far should a doctor go in trying to save life? Is he justified in doing all he can to save the suffering of a man who has an incurable disease, from which he will soon die? Should he ever give a man in dreadful pain and near to death, a dose of powerful drugs which, while alleviating the pain, is slowly killing the patient?

Some people think that a law should be passed allowing a doctor to kill those suffering from an incurable disease. What do you think?

If you think he should be allowed to do this, who should make the decision as to whether or not the patient should die? The doctor? The nearest relative? The patient? Has any man the right to say that his doctor can kill him?

Find out all you can about the early use of chloroform in surgery, and also about other anaesthetics for example, the use of Nitrous Oxide, (laughing gas) in dentistry.

A Prayer

O Lord, help me to alleviate suffering in the world, from whatever source it comes.

For further reading

Cartwright, F.F.   Joseph Lister, the Man who made Surgery Safe
                                                    Wiedenfeld and Nicholson
Jones, Howard   Men of Courage   Bell and Sons
Wymer, Norman   Medical Scientists and Doctors (Lives of Great Men & Women)
                                                                    O.U.P.
Williams-Ellis, Annabel Men Who Found Out   Bodley Head

WILLIAM MOMPESSON

The year was 1665. London was in the grip of the Great Plague. It had spread rapidly because of the lack of adequate drainage and sanitation in the City. Domestic refuse of all kinds, piled up in the middle of the narrow streets, helped to pollute the area quickly. Hundreds died, and had to be buried in large communal graves. At dead of night, horses pulling creaking carts could be heard clattering up the cobbled London Streets, and as the carters called out, "Bring out your dead!" relatives would carry out the dead bodies and place them on the top of the pile of corpses in the carts. It was a dreadful time, and people naturally lived in great fear of catching the disease.

In the middle of the epidemic, a parcel of cloth was sent from London to a tailor in the little village of Eyam, in Derbyshire, 150 miles away. Disease germs in the cloth caused the tailor and his family to become ill with the plague, and a few days later the whole family was dead. During the ensuing weeks, other villagers caught the disease and died. Some began to panic, and contemplated leaving the stricken village.

The Vicar of Eyam, the Rev. William Mompesson, now realised that he must lead his flock to do what he knew to be right. If people left the village, the disease could easily spread far and wide. There was only one course of action. Everyone must agree to stay where he was, and no-one from outside must be allowed to enter. The Vicar rallied the villagers, and secured their co-operation for his plan. All saw the sense of what he wanted them to do. In addition, everyone helped everyone else by taking turns with feeding the sick, or nursing, or burying the dead.

For four long months Eyam was completely cut off from the outside world. Food was placed by well-wishers outside the village, to be collected at night. By the time the outbreak had subsided, two hundred and fifty nine out of the three hundred villagers had died, and this number included the Vicar's wife.

But the plague did not spread from Eyam. The brave villagers through their selfless action, had saved many others from death.

In the following year, much of London was burned to the ground in the Great Fire of 1666. The new London which arose from the ashes of the Great Fire was better planned than the old City, and much wiser provision was made for sanitation.

To think about

Would we be prepared to sacrifice ourselves, even at the cost of death, in order to save others? If we had been in Eyam during the Plague, should we have been content to stay where we were, to face almost certain death? Or should we have tried to escape?

There have been many examples in history of people who have put others first, and themselves last. Can one do such a thing without believing in God? Does a belief in God help us to make right decisions when faced with a crisis like this?

A Prayer

O Lord, when the pressure is on, help me to face up to the issues, no mater how difficult that may be; and help me never to be afraid to stand up and be counted in any righteous cause.

For further reading

Fox, E.	London in Peril	Butterworth
Murphy, E.J.	Samuel Pepys in London	Longman

SIR ISAAC NEWTON

Newton was one of the greatest scientists the world has produced. He was born in Woolsthorpe, Lincolnshire, on Christmas Day, 1642, and educated at Grantham, where a statue of him stands to this day. Newton's father had died before he was born, but when the young boy was three his mother married again, leaving her son in the care of her mother.

Isaac was a short figure, with a broad forehead, a square jaw, a prominent nose and blue eyes. He was always a very honest boy, and deeply religious. At first he was not a good scholar, but a fight with another boy, which Newton won, seemed to mark the turning-point of his life, for he became the brightest boy in the school!

He entered Trinity College, Cambridge, in 1661, but four years later, owing to the outbreak of the Great Plague, he moved for two years. In 1668 he returned to Cambridge, having been elected to a College fellowship. He remained here for almost the next thirty years, buried in the researches which made him famous. In 1696 he left Cambridge, moving to London, where he held positions in the Mint.

One is able, in a short review of this wonderful man's life to give only the briefest glimpse of his wonderful mathematical and scientific discoveries. Early in his adult life he made important developments in certain branches of Mathematics. He also experimented with white light, showing that it is made up of all the colours of the rainbow. Much of his work was connected with lenses and prisms, and Newton invented the reflecting telescope, still often called the Newtonian telescope. He also invented a microscope and a sextant. Many honours from learned societies were bestowed upon him.

But perhaps his greatest discoveries were connected with the motions of the heavenly bodies in space, and he deduced from his experiments the pull of gravity, which holds the moon in its orbit. Newton did not profess to know the reason for gravity; he gave to Science his theory free from any guesswork as to what caused the phenomena he had observed.

His writing considerably enhanced his reputation, and many of the developments of modern science can be traced back to his "Mathematical Principles of Natural Philosophy".

In 1727 he became very ill, and died on March 20th. He was buried in Westminster Abbey.

Although Newton was always profoundly religious, he kept his beliefs secret, and we know little about him in this respect. He retained a humility all his life. He once said of himself, "I do not know what I may appear to the world, but to myself I seem to have been only like a boy playing on the sea-shore... while the great ocean of truth lay all undiscovered before me."

To think about:

It is often said that Science and Religion don't mix, and that Science can refute the claims of Religion. Yet we hear much more from the scientists who deny Religion than from those who support it. Why? Probably because anything controversial is newsworthy, and anything uncontroversial is not. Many of our most prominent scientists today would certainly not deny a religious interpretation of life. Large numbers would agree with Newton that important new discoveries only reveal how much more still remains to be discovered, and that with all his knowledge, Man isn't as clever as he sometimes thinks himself to be.

A Prayer:

O God, we thank You for our great scientists, who are able to unlock some of the great secrets of the Universe. The more we discover, the more we stand in awe of Your wonderful creation. Help us always to understand that Man is never able to work out his own salvation without Your help, and the help of Your Son, Jesus Christ, whose life was spent not in scientific discovery, but in showing us how to live in harmony with each other, and with You.

For further reading:

The Dictionary of National Biography has a very full entry on Isaac Newton.

Rattansi, P.M.   Isaac Newton & Gravity   Priory Press

JOHN NEWTON

Many people have experienced at some time in their lives a dramatic confrontation with Jesus Christ, and their lives are transformed from that moment onwards. St. Paul's life was changed in a moment of time on the road to Damascus. Another man who became a wonderful servant for Christ following his conversion was John Newton.

He was born in London in 1725, and went to sea on his father's ship at the age of eleven. Life at sea was hard, and later, after Newton had been forced to join a man o'war, he was publicly flogged for trying to escape. Later he went to Africa where he was employed by a slave dealer, and for a time he was Captain of a slave ship. He was a thoroughly wicked character, noted particularly for his vile language.

One day in 1748, while Newton was at sea, a terrific thunderstorm broke. The ship was in grave danger of sinking. During this time of danger, Newton's wicked past flashed before him, and, filled with remorse, he vowed that if he was spared he would dedicate the whole of his future life to God.

He was spared, and true to his word he began to prepare himself for the life of a clergyman. In 1764 he was ordained a priest by the Bishop of Lincoln, and he was made Curate at Olney in Buckinghamshire.

Together with his friend William Cowper the poet, Newton compiled a book of hymns. Newton's contributions included "How sweet the name of Jesus sounds", and also "Glorious things of Thee are spoken", which we often sing to Haydn's beautiful tune. Newton even helped William Wilberforce with his campaign to abolish slavery. He was completely changed; a new man in Christ.

In recent years his great hymn "Amazing Grace" has become very popular. In it, Newton describes something of the great change that took place in his life when he accepted Christ as his Saviour.

1. Amazing grace! How sweet the sound
   That saved a wretch like me!
   I once was lost, but now am found;
   Was blind, but now I see.

2. 'Twas grace that taught my heart to fear
   And grace my fears relieved;
   How precious did that grace appear,
   The hour I first believed.

3. Through many dangers, toils and snares,
   I have already come

'Tis grace that brought me safe thus far,
And grace will lead me home.

4. Yes, when this heart and flesh shall fail,
   And mortal life shall cease,
   I shall possess, within the veil,
   A life of joy and peace.

To think about:
Think of the power that changed John Newton from a wicked man to a disciple of Christ! Many thousands of people have also been changed dramatically by a sudden confrontation with their Saviour. If love is not at work in the world, what other power could be responsible for these changes? Read of the dramatic confrontation of St. Paul with Jesus in the Acts of the Apostles, Chapter 9, and of how Paul was changed from being a persecutor of Christians into one of Christ's most wonderful apostles.

A Prayer:
God be merciful to me, a sinner. Help me always to keep before me the image of Jesus Christ and His wonderful love for me; and help me to respond to that love by living only for Him.

For further reading:

Martin, B.   John Newton   Heinemann
Borer, Mary Cathcart   Famous Rogues   Longmans

FLORENCE NIGHTINGALE

Florence Nightingale, born on 12th May 1820 in Florence, Italy (from which city she took her name) was the second daughter of a rich country gentleman. She need never have worked for her living, and her mother would have liked her to marry into the Society of the day, but Florence was not the kind of person to live in idleness and she yearned to dedicate her life to some Christian purpose. At the age of 17 she heard the voice of God calling her to a life of service. She decided on nursing, but her parents were shocked, because in those days nurses were recruited from among ignorant women, who were frequently drunken and of low moral standard. It was unheard of for an educated woman to take up nursing.

But her iron will gradually broke down her family's resistance and when she was 31 years old she entered a convent in Germany for training. She later went to hospitals in London, Edinburgh and Paris.

In March 1854 the Crimean War was declared, and soldiers from Britain were sent to help the Turks fight the Russians. The British force was ill-equipped, and very little preparation had been made for the wounded, who died at an alarming rate. Florence Nightingale read of the appalling conditions, and volunteered to go to help. She set sail with thirty-eight nurses, and was given full charge of the Military Hospital at Scutari. Conditions there were dreadful; no sanitation and no clean garments. Wounded men were lying around in conditions of indescribable filth. The food was bad. But the worst problem faced by Florence was that she was resented by the military authorities, who opposed all her attempts to improve conditions.

Her strong determination and powers of organisation were needed to the full to put things right, and she worked tirelessly, often for twenty hours a day, for the well-being of the soldiers in hospital. Long after all her nurses were in bed, she would walk quietly through the wards to see that all was well. She had a special word of solace for those she thought needed comforting the most. As she went on her rounds, she carried her lamp, and she became known among the soldiers as, "The Lady of the Lamp".

As a result of her efforts, the numbers of deaths in the hospital went down dramatically, and after the War she was acclaimed everywhere as a heroine. But the hard work at Scutari had taken its toll; she was now a semi-invalid for the rest of her life.

Her methods of hospital management and training of nurses have left a mark on the English nursing service which will never be forgotten. She, more than anyone else, made Nursing what it is today, an honourable profession for dedicated people.

In 1907, in her old age, Florence was awarded the Order of Merit by King Edward VII. By that time she had been in retirement for so long that many people thought she had been dead for some years.

She died on 13th August 1910, and at her request was buried in family grave in Hampshire, rather than in Westminster Abbey, as had been offered to her.

To think about:

What do you think it is that makes people shun well-paid prospects in life, and take up work like nursing?

Which do you think is the more important in your working life, to acquire as much money as possible, or to choose work which you think will give you the greatest satisfaction?

A Prayer:

Help me, O Lord, throughout my life, to see clearly the things that really matter, and not just the things which at first appear to be the most attractive.

For further reading:

Davey, C.	Lady with a Lamp: Florence Nightingale (Faith and Fame Series)	
		Lutterworth
Delgado, A.	As They Saw Her – Florence Nightingale	Harrap
Stewart, P.	Florence Nightingale	Wayland

CAPTAIN OATES

In the year 1912, in the long Antarctic day, five men stood in silence at the South Pole. Captain Robert Falcon Scott, father of Peter Scott, a wildlife personality sometimes on television, had arrived there with four of his explorers after a weary journey over frozen wastes, to find that another explorer, the Norwegian Captain Amundsen had beaten him to his goal by only a few weeks.

Scott and his men were bitterly disappointed, as they had hoped to win the unofficial race to be first at the South Pole. With heavy hearts, they turned back to retrace their steps to their main base, which was a hundred and fifty miles away.

The return journey, right from the start, seemed much harder than the outward march. The men plodded on, dragging their sledges across mile after mile of the windswept wilderness of ice and snow. The biting wind made them numb with cold, in spite of their thick clothing. Sometimes they were unable to locate the tracks they had made on the outward journey, as these had been covered with fresh snow. They could not stray from their original track, in case they were unable to locate the food they had left behind.

Food was getting short, and the next depot was still some distance away. Now the wind increased to hurricane force. One man's fingers became badly frostbitten. But worse was to come. Captain Lawrence Edward Grace Oates (known to his friends as Titus), one of the party, tried to keep cheerful. He was used to doing this in the face of adversity, as he had fought in the Boer War and had been seriously wounded there.

But his smile hid a dreadful secret. His feet were badly frostbitten, and every step he took was sheer agony for him.

Later in the tiny tent, with the wind flapping the canvas violently, Oates came face to face with the biggest decision of his life. As an Army man, he had often had to make hard decisions, but never one quite like this. Would he stick with his friends, and hinder their progress, or would he stay behind, knowing that it meant certain death for him? He thought in silence for a time, and then announced in a quiet voice that he was going out of the tent for a walk.

His three companions knew just what he meant, but they said nothing. They had sensed for some time that Oates was unable to carry on by himself. He crawled slowly through the tent flap, and bent his head into the teeth of the blizzard. After a few agonising steps, he fell. The snow quickly covered his body, and he perished.

It was March 17th, his birthday. In the vast, empty wastes of Antarctica, Oates had given his comrades his life to try to save them. As a Christian, he had been guided in the hour of his testing by the words of Jesus, "Greater love hath no man than this, that a man lay down his life for his friends".

All the party later perished. Captain Scott, referring to Captain Oates's great sacrifice, wrote in his diary with a freezing, trembling hand: "So died a very gallant gentleman".

To think about:

What do you think of people who risk their lives to get to places where no-one had ever been before? Are they fools or heroes? What value is there, for example, in climbing a hitherto-unscaled mountain? Is it right that other men should have to risk their lives to rescue those who have been trapped on a mountain where they need never have ventured? One mountaineer, when asked why he wanted to climb the unconquered peak, replied simply, "Because it's there!" What do you think about this answer?

A Prayer:

O Lord, make me never to be afraid to accept life's challenges. Give me courage when my conscience tells me to do something, even though it may be hard to do.

For further reading:

Warren, C. Henry   Great Men of Essex   Pitman

LOUIS PASTEUR

Pasteur, born at Dôle in France on 27th December 1822, the son of a tanner, gave his life to conquering disease. he was interested in bacteria, the little organisms which exist in the air, in our bodies, in the soil and in water. Many of these bacteria work for the good of man, but others cause disease.

Louis studied hard as a young man, and he later held scientific posts in French provincial towns and also in Paris.

He became convinced that bacteria travel through the air from place to place. He proved his point by heating some broth, and then protecting it from the open air in special flasks. The broth did not go mouldy, as did similar broth which had been left exposed to the open air. Further experiments showed that fresh air contained far fewer bacteria than air from stuffy rooms. He went on to show that the fermentation of wine and milk was due to micro-organisms existing in the air.

Pasteur's name is perpetuated in the word "Pasteurisation", for he discovered that harmful bacteria in milk could be rendered harmless if the liquid was heated to a certain temperature. Today, all pasteurised milk is treated in this way.

He then investigated a disease which was on the point of destroying the French silkworm industry. By locating the guilty bacteria, he was able to get rid of the problem.

Next he turned his attention to a disease called anthrax, which can be fatal, and which human beings can catch if wounds come into contact with the bristle or hair of infected animals. Pasteur noticed that cows never caught anthrax twice, and this led him to wonder whether an injection of weak anthrax germs would give animals protection from the full force of the disease. Further experiments proved his ideas to be correct. He was widely acclaimed for the discovery.

The same basic discovery was now applied by Pasteur to a disease called rabies, which can be caught by human beings from the bite of an infected dog. Again, he was able to show that an injection of weak germs conferred immunity from a full attack of the disease. He also prepared vaccines against fowl cholera and diphtheria.

In spite of the great value to Mankind of his discoveries, Pasteur chose to remain a poor man and to lead a simple life. But money raised by public subscription led to the formation of the Pasteur Institute in Paris.

On the occasion of his seventieth birthday, this great scientist received honours from all over the scientific world. Always a deeply religious man, he lived on to the age of 75, and died on 28th September 1895. He is remembered as one of the greatest scientists of all time.

To think about:

Make a list of diseases for which a cure still has to be found. Find the names of doctors and scientists other than Louis Pasteur who have helped to save life by conquering disease. Read the story of Alexander Fleming, the discoverer of penicillin, the biggest life-saver of all time. What are the essential qualities, do you think, for a doctor or scientist who is trying to find a cure for a disease to possess? Would it help if he were a Christian? If so, why?

A Prayer:

O God, give us we pray Thee the desire to know You a little better each day, as we discover at school more and more about you and Your wonderful world.

For further reading:

Burton, Mary Jane	Louis Pasteur – Founder of Microbiology	
		Chatto & Windus
Pain, N.	Louis Pasteur	Black
Winner, H.J.	Louis Pasteur & Microbiology	Priory Press
Serjeant, R.	Louis Pasteur and the Fight against Disease	Macdonald
Wymer, Norman	Medical Scientists and Doctors (Lives of Great Men)	
		O.U.P.
Mann, A.L. & Vivian, C.	Famous Biologists	Museum Press
Williams-Ellis, Annabel	Men Who Found Out	Bodley Head

CHARLES PEAN

Charles Pean was born in Paris, but his father died when he was young, and the boy left his native land to live in Algeria, which was a part of the French Empire. Most of his childhood was spent on his wealthy uncle's estate in Algeria, and here he was attracted to Christianity.

Later he attended an agricultural college in France, and while still a student he came into contact with the Salvation Army. He grew to have a high esteem for the organisation and the work it was doing, and this in turn made him long to become a full-time worker for the Salvation Army. After training, he was commissioned in 1920. For five years he worked for the Army in Paris and Marseilles, two large cities with plenty of social problems to occupy his time.

In 1928 he was sent out by the Salvation Army to find out more about life and conditions in a notorious convict settlement in South America called Devil's Island. The French had a large tract of land named French Guiana, on the north coast of South America, and there were difficulties in the middle of the nineteenth century in obtaining cheap labour to work on the farms in the Colony. Slavery was now abolished, so the French Government hit upon the idea of transporting convicts from France to do the work. In 1852, 2,200 convicts were transported to the steaming jungles of French Guiana, many never to return. Some were guilty of only minor offences.

Among the convicts there were murderers, and men who were habitual criminals. There were also political prisoners, who were housed on Devil's Island, twenty miles off the coast. After completion of their prison sentences these men were not allowed to return home for a term equal to their original sentence, and many turned to crime during these periods. The result of this penal system was that all convicts dreaded going to French Guiana, and especially to Devil's Island. It was a living hell, where cruelty and beatings were commonplace.

The Salvation Army sent Charles Pean to investigate conditions on Devil's Island in 1928. He received a great welcome from both prisoners and the Governor, who, perhaps rather surprisingly, asked Pean to do all he could when he returned to France to close the convict settlement. This was surely proof of the unsatisfactory conditions prevailing there, if indeed proof were needed.

Five years later Pean returned with other Salvation army officers to the penal settlement, and they spared no effort to help the unfortunate men to lead normal lives. Help was especially needed by those who had completed their sentence but who were not allowed for the time being to return home. A house with a recreation hall and carpenter's shop was built for them, farms were started, and savings schemes were introduced so that the ex-convicts could buy tickets back to France. Once back in their native land, the ex-prisoners were helped to find work, and somewhere to live.

The help was not easy to organise among hardened individuals. Some of them could still be violent, and very unreliable. But some responded to the lessons in Christianity, and the example in Christian living, given by the Salvation Army officers.

Just before World War II the French Government promised to close the settlement, and by 1952 the dreaded Devil's Island and the French convict prisons in South America were just a memory.

To think about:

Devil's Island, like other convict settlements in the world in the last century, was a dreadful place, where brutality and disease combined with steaming heat to make life extremely uncomfortable. It is easy to say, "Well, the convicts have all deserved it, so they have no one to blame but themselves", and to turn a blind eye to it all. It is not so easy to realise that however brutal and degraded these men might be, whatever crimes they might have committed, they are all God's creatures, and that Christians have a duty to help them to try to change their lives. Charles Pean was a brave Christian who tried to do just that. What should we have done in similar circumstances?

A Prayer:

O God, help us never to turn away from our unfortunate fellow-men and women, no mater how much they have done wrong to others. Teach us that it is our duty to help everyone, whether we want to or not, whether we like it or not. And just as Jesus forgave those who had wronged Him, help us to forgive those who do wrong to us. Amen.

For further reading:
Brian Peachment   Devil's Island – Charles Pean
                                        Religious Education Press

ST. PERPETUA

In the days of ancient Rome, some of the Emperors persecuted the Christians because they insisted on putting their God, rather than the Emperor, first. Some of the worst persecutions took place under the Emperor Nero. When a fire broke out in Rome in A.D. 64, Nero blamed the Christians for it, and used it as an excuse to kill many of them by the most horrible deaths he could devise.

Many Christians died in the sporting arenas. Crowds used to go to these places to see fights to the death between gladiators, but sometimes spectators would be given additional items of entertainment, in the form of Christians being killed for their beliefs. History records many stories of Christians who died bravely in the amphitheatres, the crowds cheering madly as wild beasts, starved for the occasion, did their worst to the innocent, helpless victims.

One such story is that of the immortal Vivia Perpetua, aged 22, the wife of a man of good position and the mother of a young baby. She was imprisoned with five others for refusing to say that she did not believe in Jesus Christ. One of those imprisoned with her was Saturus, her Christian instructor. The Emperor Severus had forbidden people to belong to the Christian sect, and he had enforced his decree with severe punishments for any who disobeyed.

Perpetua's father was persuaded to come and plead with her to renounce her faith, but she would not be moved. At her trial she made no secret to the judge, Hilarian, of the fact that she was a Christian. She was therefore condemned to be sent to the arena at Carthage, to face the worst a savage cow could do.

Perpetua and others like her walked to their death with radiant faces, singing a psalm of triumph. She and another Christian girl named Felicitas went forward together, and were charged and tossed by the snorting animal. They dragged themselves to their feet, and waited for the next part of their ordeal. Perpetua's young brother managed to speak to her during this pause in the proceedings, but Perpetua told him not to be concerned for her, as she knew full well what she was doing. All the time the crowd were screaming for more "sport". One of the gladiators then took a sword, and, in full view of the crowd, killed the Christians. Perpetua guided his sword to her throat. It was 7th March, A.D. 203.

Horrible as this story is, the remarkable thing was that the number of Christians in the Roman Empire grew under the persecutions. People rightly thought that if these brave men and women were prepared to die for their faith, there must be something in what they believed.

Persecution of the Christians in the Roman Empire stopped with the Emperor Constantine.

To think about:
Try to find the names of other Christians who died under the Roman persecutions. Find out all you can about the Emperor Nero, and of his treatment of the Christians.

If those early Christians had been afraid to stand up, and if necessary to die, for their faith, what would have been the historical consequences, do you think?

Find out what you can about the suppression of Christianity under Communism in the present century.

A Prayer:
O Lord, we give our thanks to all those brave souls who have been prepared to suffer and to die for Thee, thus setting us a glorious example. Help each of us to be brave in times of danger.

For further reading:
Walker, Vera C. A First Church History Student Christian Movement Press

CLIFF RICHARD

Cliff – real name Harry Webb – was born in Lucknow, India, in 1940. His father was Area Manager for a firm called Kelner's. The family left for England in 1947, when India obtained Home Rule.

In this country, the family lived with relatives for a time, but later moved to a council house at Cheshunt. Mr Webb found employment as a Clerk.

Cliff's first English school was at Carshalton. He proved to be an average scholar, but at times in his life he showed no interest whatever in Religious Education; in fact the subject left him cold.

When he left school, he fell under the spell of Elvis Presley, whose rock music was sweeping the country. Cliff's first job was as a Clerk, but singing fascinated him, and he hadn't left school long before he had signed a record contract. About this time he adopted his professional name, which was always associated with his group of musicians, then known at The Drifters. The group later changed its name to The Shadows, and they had many engagements, both at home and overseas.

It was at about this time Cliff's father died. Cliff loved him, but had always looked upon him as a stern figure, who just wouldn't let his son do any job that he could do himself. But the death of his father was a great shock to Cliff and his three sisters, and, of course, to Mrs Webb, who later married again.

Although Cliff had by now achieved considerable success and fame, he somehow felt that there was something vital missing in his life. He was unfulfilled. The idea struck him that he would try to contact his father through a spirit medium, in an effort to discover why he was not getting all he felt he should from life. But a friend warned him against dabbling in the spirit world. He subsequently looked into Jehovah's Witnesses, but later found complete fulfilment in a deep, personal Christian faith, after a period of heartsearching. The moment of decision came for him after a Whitsun camp, where important Christian issues were argued out with friends. Now there was no looking back.

But there were still many problems to solve, in particular about reconciling Christianity with his chosen career of pop music. As a Christian, his priorities in life were now different, and his standards needed constant vigilance. He was invited to many meetings to talk about his commitment to Christianity, and admits he sometimes felt inadequate to answer some of the searching questions that were put to him. In addition, his motives were often misrepresented in the press.

He now began to take a special interest in Tear Fund, an organisation formed by Christians to enable fellow-Christians to give practical help to those in desperate need in poor countries – earthquake victims, those who were suffering from starvation and disease, the homeless, etc. Cliff visited some of the countries where these unfortunate human beings lived – Bangladesh, the Sudan, Kenya and

Haiti among them – and the suffering he saw went straight to his heart. He has given many concerts to raise money for Tear Fund.

Another charity in which he is very interested is the Arts Centre Group, through which Christians involved in the Arts – the stage, music, films, etc. – can meet and talk. Wide gulfs often exist between the Arts and the Church, and the Arts Centre Group endeavours to explore and encourage points of contact.

Cliff always strives for the highest standards of professionalism in his work, and it is indeed remarkable that his popularity has not waned after so many years in show business. But in spite of his wonderful success, which has earned him the award of the O.B.E., and the chance to meet many famous people, including royalty, he still maintains a sense of values by making God his top priority at all times.

To think about:

Money, success, screaming fans – all these have come to Cliff Richard for many years. By all worldly standards he is a complete success. And yet Cliff knows that there is more to life than this. He searched for a real meaning of life, which encompasses those who are underprivileged, starving and homeless. By identifying himself with an organisation dedicated to helping these unfortunate people, Cliff finds a deep and lasting happiness such as the world of pop music, by itself, can never bring.

A Prayer:

O God, help us all to understand, as we make our way in the world, that money and success are not an end in themselves. May we never forget that You sent Your Son into the world to show us the real meaning of life, and that this is only to be found by loving You, and by loving our neighbour.

For further reading:

Which One's Cliff?	(Cliff's autobiography)	Coronet Books, 1981
You, Me, and Jesus.	Cliff Richard	Hodder & Stoughton, 1983
Mine to Share	Cliff Richard	Hodder & Stoughton, 1984

SIR ERNEST SHACKLETON

Sir Ernest Shackleton was one of the most intrepid explorers of all time. Born at Kilkee, Ireland, on 15th February 1874, he made an excursion to the Antarctic regions under Captain Scott in 1901. Later, in 1907, he commanded another expedition to the South Polar regions, and this time his party climbed Mount Erebus, the Antarctic volcano (13,000 ft. approx), and also reached the South Magnetic Pole. At one point the party was less than a hundred miles from the South Pole itself.

He made a gallant but unsuccessful attempt to cross the Antarctic Continent in another expedition in 1914. His ship, the Endurance, was crushed in the pack-ice of the Weddell Sea, and this unfortunate episode spelt the end of the attempt to cross the frozen wasteland. Shackleton and his men drifted northwards on heaving ice floes which sometimes split as they thawed in the warmer water. On one occasion, as the men slept in their tents on an ice floe, a great split in the floe passed right through the middle of the tent. The men inside had to grab their belongings and quickly jump to safety across an ever-widening gap of icy water.

Eventually the party all took to the smaller boats they had taken from the Endurance, and made for Elephant Island, an uninhabited and cheerless place where, fortunately, there was bird life which could be used for food.

Shackleton and five of his most trusted men now decided to attempt to cross in a small boat the wildest stretch of ocean in the world, in an effort to reach help at the whaling station on South Georgia, 800 miles away. They said farewell to their friends who were remaining behind on Elephant Island. All had the utmost faith in their leader's ability to get through.

Mountainous seas and severe squalls gave the little boat a severe battering, but Shackleton fought through and arrived at isolated South Georgia only to find that he had landed on the side of the island which was opposite to the whaling station. The men pulled the little boat on to the deserted beach, and set out on foot to cross the mountainous, snow-covered interior of the island, which had never been traversed by man. At last they burst into the huts of the startled whalers, who immediately offered help.

Three attempts had to be made by sea to reach the men left behind on Elephant Island; but the faith of the men in their "boss" had never faltered. Every day they had prepared for his return by rolling up their sleeping bags and packing their few belongings. They were always ready to depart at a moment's notice.

Shackleton was himself a Christian. While he was crossing the uncharted mountains of South Georgia, he records that he felt all the time that someone was by his side, leading him, guiding him onwards.

The small boat in which Shackleton and his men crossed the wild Scotia Sea, from Elephant Island to South Georgia, was later brought to England, and can today be seen at his old school, Dulwich College London.

Shackleton was knighted in 1909 and died on 5th January 1922. He is buried on South Georgia.

To think about:

What was it about Shackleton's character, do you think, that made the men who were stranded on Elephant Island believe so implicitly in his power to get through and to bring help?

Shackleton was a Christian. Others, who are not Christians, also do great feats of daring. Do you think that being a Christian helped Shackleton in any way during his terrible sea voyage in the open boat from Elephant Island to South Georgia? If so, how did it help him?

A Prayer:

O Lord, Whenever a challenge that I feel I must accept confronts me in this life, give me the strength to accept it and to win through with determination.

For further reading:

Smith, B. Webster   Sir Ernest Shackleton   Blackie

Warner, Oliver   Great seamen from Drake to Cunningham
     Bell (Chapter 6)

THE EARL OF SHAFTESBURY

Lord Ashley, born 28th April 1801, became the Earl of Shaftesbury and gave a lifetime of service to his less-fortunate countrymen. As an evangelical Christian, he was ruled by the conviction that Christian conduct should enter into every aspect of life. To him his religion was far more important than personal ambition. There were a great number of social evils to be tackled in the middle of the nineteenth century, but it was the sight of a pauper's funeral, with all its degradation and poverty, that so moved Ashley that he determined to devote himself to the service of the poor.

One of his first acts was in connection with men and women of unsound mental condition, who were considered as social outcasts and who were locked away. Ashley urged much more humane treatment for them, and his efforts were crowned with success in the Lunacy Act of 1845.

Those who have read Charles Kingsley's "Water Babies" will know something of the evils of boys sweeping chimneys in the eighteenth and early nineteenth centuries. The chimneys of the rich often twisted, and could not be swept clean with a brush, so poor little urchins were forced by brutal masters to climb them, cleaning as they went. It needs little imagination to picture their smarting eyes and their throats choked with soot. In 1840, after a valiant fight, Ashley succeeded in persuading the Government to bring in a Bill prohibiting the employment of child sweeps, though more legislation followed later.

Next he turned his attention to the coal mines, where men, women and children often worked in fearful conditions. Girls often wore round their waists a stout belt of leather, attached to which was a heavy piece of iron chain. The other end of the chain was fastened to a loaded coal truck. On hands and knees the girls would pull the trucks, often up steep inclines, in subterranean roads perhaps only two feet high. The Mines Act of 1842 put a stop to this inhuman treatment of children; from now on it was illegal for women and children to work in the mines.

An Act in 1847, pressed through by Ashley, limited the hours of work of women and young people in factories to ten a day. Up to that time it had been a common sight to see young boys and girls fall asleep with fatigue while at their machines in the factories.

Many other reforms were due to Lord Ashley. He helped to found schools for poor children, and he was always keenly concerned with housing conditions, water supply, and provision for sanitation – in short, with everything connected with the lives of the underprivileged.

The statue of Eros, in Piccadilly Circus, in London, is perhaps rather strangely, intended as a memorial to Lord Shaftesbury, who is numbered among the greatest of our social reformers.

He died on 1st October 1885, at Folkestone.

To think about:

Read all you can about the harsh treatment of children at work in this country in the early part of the nineteenth century. Try to find out about the work of the N.S.P.C.C.. Read Charles Dickens' "Oliver Twist" for descriptions of life in the workhouse for homeless boys in the nineteenth century. Can you suggest why conditions should be so very hard for so many poor people in Britain in the last century.

A Prayer:

Lord, we thank You for all those men and women who have fought to make better the lives of children in this country and throughout the world. Help us never to be afraid to stand up for those who need help.

For further reading:

Chambers, Peggy	They Fought for Children	Wyman and Sons (p23)
Evans, J.O.	Benefactors of the World	Frederick Warne (p41)
Jones, Howard	Men of Courage	Bell and Sons

SAINT STEPHEN

Stephen was, as far as we know, the first man to die for Christ; the first Christian martyr.

One day, the Apostles of Jesus came to Stephen and said that they were looking for seven men to help them with their work of preaching and healing. The work of these seven would be to look after the money which the Apostles collected for sick people, and also to do some preaching.

Stephen was an excellent, forthright preacher, and he knew that many of the Jews wouldn't like what he said. Some of the important Jews hoped that Jesus would be forgotten now that He had been crucified, but here was a man determined to perpetuate His memory and the truths He had come to proclaim. When he spoke, Stephen pulled no punches, and many of the things he said stung his enemies. In the end, his Jewish enemies sent for Stephen and debated with him to try to prove that Jesus was not what Stephen claimed Him to be. But Stephen was more than a match for them in debate and argument, so they hauled him before the Sanhedrin, the Jewish Council. Again Stephen spoke out fearlessly, and testified that Jesus was the Son of God.

The members of the Sanhedrin were filled with anger. They literally dragged Stephen out of the Chamber, and pulled him through the crowded streets. They dared not harm him while he was inside the City, as permission had to be obtained from the Roman Governor to put anyone to death. But once he was outside the City, no-one could save him.

As Stephen was dragged along, crowds followed, and the Jews whipped up the feeling of the crowd against him. When he was outside the City gates, they stood him against a wall and proceeded to stone him to death. Stephen made no protest as the heavy stones struck him. In fact, he cried out, "Lord, lay not this sin to their charge".

So died Stephen, the first Christian martyr. One of those who watched the whole proceedings was Saul, who was later known as Paul. We may guess that Saul was impressed at the sight of this man forgiving his enemies as the stones rained down upon him. Not long afterwards, Saul was on his way to Damascus to persecute the Christians there, when he had a vision, which transformed him, and he became a mighty worker for Jesus Christ.

To think about:
Jesus said, "Love your enemies; bless them that curse you; pray for them that despitefully use you". He also said "Unto him that smiteth thee on the one cheek, offer also the other". How far can we take this as a code of conduct to be strictly observed in our daily lives? Would the world be a better place if we did this, or would some people take advantage of us for what they saw as our stupidity? Would all wars cease if Christians followed these words of Jesus? or would non-Christian enemies think that we were just mad?

Stephen forgave his enemies as the stones fell upon him. What does it need in a man to be able to do this? Could we ever visualise ourselves doing the same?

A Prayer:
Lord, help us to capture in our lives something of the goodness of Stephen as he forgave his enemies. Help us to understand that loving is always better, and always stronger, than hating, and that You came on earth to teach us to love each other, and to love God, our Heavenly Father.

For further reading:

Mary Cousins   Tell me about the Saints   Hutchinson

SIR PHILIP SIDNEY

Sir Philip Sidney, who was born on November 30th, 1554 at Penshurst, Kent, lived in the reign of Queen Elizabeth 1st. He was a poet, scholar and soldier, but if he had been nothing more than these he would not have achieved the fame he did. He is remembered especially because he was a gentleman of great character, and also because he was a devout Christian.

He was often sent on missions for his Queen. Two years after he was knighted in 1583, he was to have gone with Sir Francis Drake on one of his expeditions, but instead he was asked to go to Holland to do what he could to help that country in its fight against Spain.

On 22nd September 1586, he fought in a battle against the Spaniards at a place called Zutphen. During a charge against the Spanish cavalry, he received a bullet wound in the leg, and lay injured on the battlefield. By the time others came to help him, he was in great pain, and very thirsty. Drinking water was very scarce but one of the soldiers had a small supply left, and he poured this into a helmet and offered it to Sir Philip for him to put to his parched lips.

As he raised the helmet, and looked at the contents with eager anticipation, Sir Philip glanced across the battlefield, and his eyes met those of another soldier, obviously very seriously wounded, who was lying on the ground not very far away. The soldier had his eyes fixed on the helmet of water. He was obviously very thirsty himself. The look on the soldier's face immediately moved Sir Philip to great compassion. He called to his side the soldier who had passed him the helmet.

"Take this to the soldier lying over there", he said, handing him the helmet. Then, to the wounded soldier, he called, "Your need is greater than mine".

The thoughts of the soldier as he quenched his parched lips are not recorded, but we may guess that the cooling water would be very gratefully received, and that he would be greatly impressed by Sir Philip's wonderful act of selflessness.

Sir Philip died at Arnhem some three weeks later, aged only thirty-two. Thousands grieved at his death, for by his great character and his virtuous Christian life he had endeared himself to people in many European countries. He was buried in St. Paul's Cathedral.

During his lifetime, he wrote several books, and these were published after his death. One of his best-known works was Arcadia, published in 1590.

To think about:
Selfishness is at the very heart of our problems today. We live in a world where very many people put their own needs before those of others, no matter what inconvenience is caused. Look at your daily newspapers and see how many of the important news items have selfishness as their cause; selfishness of individuals, selfishness of groups of people, selfishness of nations.

It has been said that selfishness in our nation has increased since so many people began to turn their backs on Christianity. How far do you think this is true?

A Prayer:
O Lord, help me, in all my actions and in all my words, to conquer my selfishness, and to live for Thee, and for other people.

For further reading:
Any good biographical dictionary or encyclopaedia.
Unstead, R.J.   Discoverers and Adventurers   A. & C. Black

CORRIE TEN BOOM

In 1939 Adolf Hitler declared war on Poland, and soon the whole of Europe was involved. German troops invaded many countries, and among these was Holland.

Hitler was obsessed with the idea that the Jewish race was responsible for most of the problems of Europe, and he made a decision to destroy as many of the European Jews as he could.

Corrie ten Boom, born between the two World Wars, lived with her sister Betsy and their father, a watchmaker, in Haarlem, in Holland. They were devout Christians, and could not bear to see Jews in their town suddenly disappear, never to return. They became involved in a plan to hide Jews, and they had a special secret room built in their house, with a system of secret warning bells in case of trouble.

Eventually they were betrayed by someone who was suspicious when he heard the warning bell, and Corrie and Betsy were taken for questioning. The father, also taken for questioning, became separated from the daughters, and died of neglect soon afterwards, and although there was a time when Corrie and Betsy might have escaped, they felt they just could not desert their Christian duty to the Jews.

The two sisters were held in custody, and after a series of detentions they were despatched in cattle trucks on a very long railway journey to one of Hitler's dreaded concentration camps, at Ravensbruck. Here they were made to exist among conditions of the greatest humiliation and degradation. The living-quarters were flea-ridden, the blankets were full of lice, and the inmates were starved and kept in cold huts. All the women prisoners had to parade naked periodically for medical checks and searches to be made.

But the two sisters never lost their faith. They looked upon their brutal guards with love, in spite of the terrible treatment meted out to them. Somehow, in spite of searches, the sisters had managed to retain their Bible, and through reading this they managed to sustain their faith and their hope.

Betsy became very ill – she was never as strong as her sister – and she died in the hospital at Ravensbruck, to the great sorrow of Corrie. But even this did not quench the spirit of this brave woman. Towards the end of the war she was released from the concentration camp, and was given some black bread and coupons for three days' rations. These were stolen, and by the time Corrie arrived back in Holland after a long railway journey she was very, very hungry.

Even now, her indomitable spirit found expression in a noble work, for after the fighting was over, in the large house of a wealthy acquaintance in Holland, she helped to rebuild the shattered lives of people who had managed to survive the horrors of war. Some had spent years in hiding from the Nazis, and others had undergone torture and untold deprivation at the hands of the Nazis.

There are so many brave stories told about Christian men and women at the hands of the Nazis, but the story of Corrie ten Boom ranks with the best. The incidents in her story are graphically portrayed in the film, "The Hiding Place".

To think about:

The treatment by Hitler of the Jewish race ranks with the very worst crimes of all times. Many people would say it was impossible for a modern civilised western nation to be responsible for killing between five and six million Jews. yet the ugly happenings inside Hitlers's concentration camps carry one great lesson for us all. If we are not watchful, we, too, can be swept off our feet by vicious propaganda, based on hate. The Bible teaches us that we are all fallen sinners, and that we are a mixture of good and evil. Life, to the Christian, consists of responding to all that which is good and true, and renouncing all that is evil. As someone once wrote:

> "There's something that pulls man upwards,
> And something that drags him down,
> And the consequence is, he wobbles,
> 'Twixt muck and a golden crown".

A Prayer:

O Lord, thank you for the life and example of Corrie ten Boom. If we are ever challenged, in times of great personal danger, may we fearlessly do what is right, for Thy dear name's sake. Amen.

For further reading:

The Hiding Place	Corrie ten Boom	Hodder & Stoughton, 1971
Amazing Love	Corrie ten Boom	Kingsway Publications 1978

MOTHER TERESA

Mother Teresa was born in Yugoslavia of Albanian parents, in 1910. She came under the influence of Christian priests at a very early age, and by the time she was twelve she was convinced that she had a calling from God to help poor people. Although her teenage years were full of doubts and uncertainties, she went to India in 1929 to teach, and in 1931 she became a nun. Ever since that time she said that her whole life has been radiantly happy, spent in the service of God and of her fellow-men and women.

Although she loved teaching, there was a small but persistent voice stirring within her. In 1946, as she was journeying to Darjeeling by train, God spoke to her again. She was to give up her work as a teacher and go into the dreadful slums of the great city of Calcutta, to work among the poorest people on earth.

Calcutta is a city of great contrasts, where rich and poor make their homes. In the mean back streets live hundreds of poor people who have no shelter at all. they live, eat, sleep and die on the pavement. For anyone who cares about suffering humanity, this is one of the most heart-rending sights in the world. Many of these destitute people are seriously ill. The Indian Government is aware of the problem, of course, but it has so many desperate social problems to tackle, and its resources are not yet enough to enable it to do all it would wish to do.

In 1948, with the Church's permission, Teresa responded to the call. After some medical training, she first gathered together some of the teenage children of the Calcutta homeless, and started a school for them. She was soon joined in her work by ladies from the school where she had formerly taught.

In 1952, she carried her work a stage further by opening, in a former heathen temple, a Home for the Dying, where desperately ill people from the streets could at least lie quietly with a roof over their heads, and receive food. The body of the first lady to be admitted was so infested with vermin that little could be done to help in a medical sense.

Many thousands of destitute people have since been given shelter. A number of those admitted were suffering from leprosy. Fortunately, a doctor volunteered for service to help the poor creatures. Those who responded to treatment were re-housed in special areas.

Similar Homes for the Dying have been opened in other cities of India, and in other countries of the world.

Mother Teresa hoped that before they die, all her patients would capture something of the Divine Love which inspired her to do this work. It is because she was doing Christ's work that she was so radiantly happy in such dreadful surroundings. But the need in the world for more work of this kind with the underprivileged masses is overwhelming.

Mother Teresa died on 5th September, 1997.

To think about:
Mother Teresa dedicated her life to the poorest, most wretched people on earth. She risked disease and death to do her work. Yet she was radiantly happy. This was doubtless partly due to her great sense of dedication in serving her less-fortunate fellow-men. But she herself said that she could not possibly sustain her work without a belief in a Higher Being to whom she could turn constantly for spiritual strength. Some would say this was just her imagination, and that others do good deeds without finding a need for God. What do you think?

A Prayer:
O Lord, give us all the dedication of Mother Teresa to work for others without thought of reward.

For further reading:
Muggeridge, Malcolm   Something Beautiful for God   Collins

WILLIAM TYNDALE

It is difficult for us to picture a time in England when Bibles were not freely available, but the Church has not always been ready to let the Scriptures be distributed among the people. This was partly because it was felt that ignorant people might misinterpret the Scriptures, and thus be led astray. Such Bibles as were in churches were not written in the English Language, and could not therefore be understood by the great mass of the people.

Many, however, thought that English Bibles ought to be freely available. One such person was William Tyndale, born in Gloucestershire in 1490, who dreamed of ordinary men and women, even to the humble ploughboy, being able to read the Gospels.

About this time there occurred an event of great importance. Martin Luther, a German priest, published a New Testament in the German language. This set Tyndale thinking again. Could he find ways and means of doing for the English people what Luther had done for the Germans? But English Church leaders were highly suspicious of his plans. There was therefore only one thing to do. He went to Germany, and never came back to his own country. He spent a year translating the New Testament into English. Then he tried to smuggle his printed copies into England. But he was soon in trouble, and English Church leaders branded his translation as erroneous in many respects. A copy of Tyndale's Bible was publicly burned as a sign to all that it was not approved by the Church.

Tyndale was very disappointed, but not altogether surprised at the official reception of his translation. He was now a hunted man, and moved from place to place to avoid arrest. He finally settled in Belgium, but was later betrayed by a man he thought was a friend, and cast into prison near Brussels. We know from Tyndale's letters that the prison was very uncomfortable, for he complains of the bitter cold.

He spent nearly a year and a half in this dreadful place, and the end came on 6th October 1536. He was taken to a public place, and, at the instigation of King Henry VIII, was strangled and burned at the stake; a martyr's death for a brave and determined man.

Tyndale's translation was so accurate, and his language was so excellent, that nine tenths of the King James version of the Bible represents Tyndale's work.

Ironically, only two years after Tyndale's death, the Archbishop of Canterbury gave instructions that every Church in England should have a copy of the Bible in English. Tyndale's work had not been in vain!

To think about:

Tyndale left his country and his friends to live overseas, because he knew that he had a mission in life which he could not fulfil here. Even so, he was imprisoned and murdered. These were dreadful times, and it took a very brave man to defy the law. Nowadays there is no persecution in this country for reading the Bible, but in the countries of the Communist world people still risk imprisonment in order to bring Bibles to the people. In some countries all reading matter is subject to censorship; and the decision as to what people shall and shall not read is a political one.

Is censorship ever justified? Should we be allowed to read <u>anything</u> that a person chooses to write? Or should <u>some</u> written material be subject to censorship to avoid obscenities appearing in print? What about reading matter that incites people to revolution? Ought that to be censored? If some censorship is necessary, who ought to do it? The Government? Would not the government be biased in choosing what should be censored, and what should not?

A Prayer:

We thank You, Lord, for brave men like Tyndale, who fought a hard battle to win men's minds and souls through the printed Word.

For further reading:

Williams, C.H.   William Tyndale   Watson & Viney
Rupp, Gordon   Six Makers of English Religion, 1500-1700
                                                    Hodder & Stoughton

WILLIAM BERNARD ULLATHORNE

William Ullathorne was the first Roman Catholic Bishop of Birmingham. He was born in Pocklington, Yorkshire, on 7th May, 1806. His father was a descendant of Sir Thomas More, the martyred Chancellor of Henry VIII, while his mother, of Protestant descent, was a cousin of Sir John Franklin, the Arctic explorer.

William showed no desire to follow in his father's drapery business, nor, as a teenager, did he show any inclination to enter the Church. But he loved to read adventure stories, particularly Robinson Crusoe, and it was this, more than any other factor, that made him eager to go to sea as a cabin boy. But later he left the sea, and joined the Benedictine monks at Downside. For a time he taught at the school at Ampleforth, Yorkshire, but this was not a successful venture on his part, so he returned to Downside. By this time he was a priest.

One day, during a journey to Bath to see a doctor, a fellow priest told him something of the dreadful plight of many of the convicts who, in those days, were transported from this country to Australia. Many were guilty of relatively small offences. Australia had been used for convicts since 1788, following the loss of the North American colonies, and the first batch of prisoners landed at Botany Bay in that year.

Ullathorne immediately volunteered to go to Australia, and he was appointed Chaplain in New South Wales. He landed in 1833. What he saw horrified him. Some prisoners were fastened together with chains, and worked in gangs. Floggings of prisoners were common. Some of the settlements were reserved for women, who, living in a state of utter hopelessness, just stagnated there. No wonder Ullathorne was so moved at the degradation and corruption that he witnessed.

Some of the convicts tried desperately to escape into the Australian bush, rather than endure the cruel regime in the settlements, but those that managed to free themselves usually died of thirst or starvation in the wilderness of inland Australia.

Ullathorne had heard of floggings taking place even in the middle of the compounds of prison hospitals, where patients were able to watch the spectacle. It appeared from his enquiries that the punishments were sometimes administered here so that dressings would be quickly available to apply to the wounds made by the floggings.

But the worst place of all was Norfolk Island, off the Australian coast where the very worst prisoners, who had committed new crimes on the mainland, were sent. Two thousand prisoners were held in captivity here, many awaiting execution. Ullathorne visited the condemned cells. Each man here was chained to a metal bar which crossed the cell from side to side. The heat in the cells was unbearable, and these conditions made many of the difficult men absolutely desperate. So tight was the security on Norfolk Island that no unauthorised ship was allowed to approach it.

When he returned to England, Ullathorne gave evidence before a Committee of Parliament about the sights he had seen in Australia. His disclosures aroused a storm of fury among officials in Australia, but Ullathorne was not deterred. He knew full well where his Christian duty lay. Opposition to the transportation system grew in this country.

Later Ullathorne worked in Coventry and Birmingham, in the latter of which he was eventually appointed Bishop. While he occupied this office, a huge meeting was held in Australia to try to erase the transportation system for ever, and in 1853 this was stopped by law.

In the 1880's Ullathorne became ill several times, eventually suffering a stroke. He died on 21st March, 1889. Death held no terrors for him. Shortly before he passed away, he said, "My mind is completely tranquil." His body lies in Stone, Staffs. Shortly before his death he had received the honorary title of Archbishop.

To think about:

A brave man gives much of his life to the investigation of an evil system, and to gathering evidence to have it stopped by law. Eventually his efforts are crowned with success, and although he was not the only person to denounce the cruel system of transportation, he was one of the most important of the men who fought for its abolition. Even though the men and women transported to Australia were criminals in the eyes of English law, they were still creatures of God, and as such Ullathorne determined to do what he could to help rescue them from a terrible, inhuman fate.

No-one wishes to make prison a life of ease and luxury, and prisons today do not give the inmates an easy time. But running alongside punishment for crime, there should surely be an attempt to reform the criminals, that is to try to make them into better people in readiness for the time when they leave prison for the outside world. Ullathorne hated the excesses of degradation and inhumanity which he saw, and his Christian conscience gave him the determination to do something about it.

A Prayer:

O Lord, help us never to tolerate evil and injustice in the world, but to do all we can as Christians to root it out. We ask this for Christ's sake. Amen.

For further reading

From Cabin Boy to Archbishop. Archbishop Ullathorne (autobiography)

Burns Oates, 1941

JOHN & CHARLES WESLEY

Samuel Wesley was Rector of Epworth in Lincolnshire, and John and Charles were two members of his large family. John had a very narrow escape from death when he was a small boy, for Epworth Rectory was burned down and John nearly perished with it.

In 1729, John and Charles started at Oxford University a discussion group for those who wished to take their Bibles very seriously. The group was known, as the "Holy Club", and sometimes as the "Bible Moths". The members prayed and studied the Scriptures in such a methodical way that they were soon dubbed "Methodists". In addition to their studies, the members of the group visited local prisons, and helped the prisoners in any way they could. They started a school for prisoners' children. Many of the prisoners were there because of crime and debt induced by drunkenness, which was very common in those days.

After release, some of the prisoners were settled in America. John and Charles went there for a time. John preached strongly against the slave trade and gin-drinking, and later came into contact with some German Protestants known as Moravians. This sect, and particularly its leader, Peter Bohler, had a profound influence on John's religious thinking, and he records that on 24th May 1738, he suddenly realised exactly where his path of duty for the rest of his life really lay. Although Wesley loved the Church of England, he knew that in some respects it was corrupt, and it seemed to neglect the spiritual needs of many of the ordinary English people. So, denied access by the Clergy to many of the Churches, he was led to preach to the poor in the open air. His first sermons were addressed to the colliers at Kingswood, Bristol, in 1739.

Thus began the most important part of John Wesley's life. For almost fifty years he travelled on horseback in England, Scotland, Ireland and Wales, in all weathers, carrying the Gospel message to the poor and forgotten. The roads in those days were little more than grass tracks, but Wesley averaged eight thousand miles and a thousand sermons each year. Sometimes he was well received; at others he was pelted with clods of earth, and attacked my mobs.

He died in 1791, aged eighty-seven, having given his nation a wonderful spiritual uplift by his noble life.

His brother Charles will always be remembered by the wonderful hymns he wrote. Hundreds of them flowed from his pen, but he is chiefly remembered for hymns like "Hark, the Herald Angels Sing", "Jesus Christ is Risen Today, Hallelujah!", "Soldiers of Christ, Arise!", "O, For a Thousand Tongues to Sing", "Love, Divine, all Loves Excelling", and "Jesu, Lover of my Soul".

To think about:

John and Charles Wesley left behind them a wonderful legacy of concern for the poor in spirit in this country, and a wonderful collection of hymns, for singing is a vital ingredient of Methodism.

How can we employ our lives and our talents so that we leave behind us something, however small, which will be of benefit to Mankind? Will it be said of us that we left behind a record of kind actions, or of kind words, to those in trouble? A record of selfless service, without reward seeking? A record of happiness in the face of adversity? Think about this.

A Prayer:

Help us, O Lord, to lead lives which are worthy of Thee, and may we hope that we shall leave the world, when our time comes, a little better place than it was when we came into it.

For further reading:

Lawson, M.	He Set Britain Aflame	Morrison & Gibb
Braislford, Mabel Richmond	John & Charles Wesley	Richard Clay
Davey, C.	Horseman of the King: John Wesley	Lutterworth
Brett, S. Reed	John Wesley	A. & C. Black

WILLIAM WILBERFORCE

Wilberforce's name will forever be associated with the fight to end slavery in the British Empire. For over a hundred years Europeans had bought slaves from Africans, and had packed them in ships and sent them to America, where they were sold in the slave markets. Often families were split up in these markets; mothers, fathers and children being bought by different masters, and never seeing each other again. Some slaves were treated kindly, but others were literally worked to death, and suffered brutal treatment.

William Wilberforce, who came from Hull and who lived from 1759 to 1833, led the opposition to slavery in this country. He was a likeable fellow, and through reading his Bible he developed a deep sense of religious conviction, becoming an evangelical Christian in 1785. He convinced his friend William Pitt, the Prime Minister, of the evils of slavery, but as it was a source of wealth to many of the members of Parliament, they refused to do anything to stop it.

Passionate speeches in Parliament on the subject of slavery were made by Wilberforce, who had become Member of Parliament for Hull in 1780, and by Pitt. Many M.P.'s were clearly moved. Even so, there was a majority of 75 for retaining slavery.

Wilberforce now pressed on with his task with renewed vigour. He went up and down the country, addressing public meetings in an effort to gain more support for his cause. His graphic descriptions of the dreadful voyages from Africa to America, with slaves shackled above and below decks as closely as they could possibly be packed together, made a big impact on many people, but those who profited from the slave trade were still very hostile towards him.

Eventually the House of Commons became convinced of the righteousness of Wilberforce's cause, and they were prepared to have a law passed to stop slavery, but in those days the House of Lords could veto whatever the Commons wished to do, and the Lords would not pass the measure.

But at last, in 1807, after untiring efforts by Wilberforce over many years, it was made illegal for British ships to carry slaves. This was no final solution to the problem however, because slave buyers simply bought slaves from foreign shipowners.

Still Wilberforce battled on, but he was now a sick man. In the year 1833, when he was on his death-bed, he heard the glad news that the British Parliament had abolished slavery in the British Empire. He died a happy man, knowing that his cause had at last triumphed.

To think about:

In spite of sickness, Wilberforce toiled with passionate endeavour for the cause in which he believed. His hour of triumph came on his death bed. He would probably have lived longer if he had taken life easily. But he has passed into history as a wonderful Christian and humanitarian. Naturally, he made many enemies in his fight to abolish slavery, but the whole of his adult life was a crusade for justice against cruel oppression. Though he would have been sorry to make enemies, he would not have been deterred on this account, because the righteousness of his cause over-rode all other considerations.

Many people are content to spend their lives in passive acceptance of the evils around them. "Anything for a quiet life" is a popular saying. What do you think?

A Prayer:

Help me, O Lord, never to accept evils which my conscience tells me are wrong. Give me strength to fight those evils which I feel I can help to stop.

For further reading:

Lawson, A. & H. The Man who Freed the Slaves –
      The Story of William Wilberforce   Faber
Johnson, Elise M. The Man who Freed Slaves   Lutterworth

JOHN LEONARD WILSON

John Wilson, born in 1898, was the son of a clergyman from Gateshead. He went to school in Leatherhead, Surrey, after which he served in World War I in the Durham Light Infantry. After the war he went to university, and subsequently entered the Ministry of the Church of England.

He served in Coventry; then as a missionary in Cairo with the Church Missionary Society; then as a Vicar in Gateshead and Monkswearmouth. Just before World War II he served in Hong Kong, and in 1941 became Bishop of Singapore.

Only a few months later the Japanese attacked, and conquered Malaya and Singapore. Bishop Wilson was taken prisoner, tortured, severely beaten, starved and placed in the infamous Changi jail in Singapore. Even in these circumstances he behaved with great courage, and when a Chinese boy, impressed by the Bishop's example, asked to be baptised into the Christian faith, the Bishop agreed, but had to use water from a lavatory pan because no other was available in prison conditions.

After the Japanese surrender in 1945, Bishop Wilson was released, much weaker and thinner for the tortures, the beatings and the starvation to which he had been subjected. He returned to England, but his first sermons displayed not the slightest trace of bitterness towards the cruel enemy, and his congregations were visibly moved by his attitude. He said he thought the Japanese did what they did because they were conditioned by their training, and because of their worship of their Emperor.

His Ministry after the war was done firstly in Manchester, but in 1953 he succeeded Dr. Barnes as Bishop of Birmingham. He was sadly missed in Manchester, where he had been described by people of widely differing religious backgrounds as a sincere man of God. He was easy to talk to, wise and farseeing in leadership, and as a war hero he was admired by many people.

Not content with "resting on his laurels", he now espoused the cause of the homeless in Birmingham, where 63,000 families were searching desperately for a place in which to live. In spite of the hastening of the end of World War II by the dropping of atomic bombs on Japan, Bishop Wilson lived in horror of another war with the use of atomic weapons, and he urged international action by the United Nations to reduce the possibility of another conflict.

His pastoral care extended to the many thousands of coloured people in the Birmingham diocese, and he once intervened to stop a strike among bus crews when a coloured driver was appointed.

Millions of people saw him on television each year, when, as a war veteran, he led the British Legion Service of Remembrance at the Royal Albert Hall.

In 1970 he suffered a severe stroke, and died on August 18th of that year. But he left behind him a wonderful record of Christian concern and service. His service on Tyneside in the 1930's had been done at a time when the area had suffered as much as any from the terrible depression of those years, but nowhere was John Wilson remembered more than in the parishes of Gateshead and Monkswearmouth where he had given such dedicated service in this testing time.

To think about:

A priest is taken prisoner by the Japanese in World War II, and is subjected to every humiliation by his captors – severe beating, torture, starvation. Yet after the war, in spite of his ordeal, he can say with Jesus, "Father, forgive them for they know not what they do." No thoughts of vengeance or retribution entered his head, but only plans for reconciliation, with a firm commitment to do all he could to see that war was outlawed for ever.

What a wonderful person, to forgive his enemies in this way! Could we find it in our hearts to do the same in similar circumstances? Or should we harbour thoughts of vengeance; of "getting our own back"?

A Prayer:

Teach us, O Lord, something of the spirit of Bishop Wilson. May we always be strong enough to forgive our enemies, as he did, and as Christ did on the cross. We ask this for Your sake. Amen.

For further reading:
An obituary in the Church times of August 21st 1970.

MOORLEY'S

We are growing publishers, adding several new titles to our list each year. We also undertake private publications and commissioned works.

Our range of publications includes:

Books of Verse:
Devotional Poetry
Recitations
Drama
Bible Plays
Sketches
Nativity Plays
Passiontide Plays
Easter Plays
Demonstrations
Resource Books
Assembly Material
Songs and Musicals
Children's Addresses
Prayers and Graces
Daily Readings
Books for Speakers
Activity Books
Quizzes
Puzzles
Painting Books
Church Stationery
Notice Books
Cradle Rolls
Hymn Board Numbers

Please send a stamped addressed envelope (approx. 9" x 6") for the current catalogue or consult your local Christian Bookshop who should stock or be able to order our titles.